THE INCREDIBLE
HUMAN BODY

ANNA BRETT

ACKNOWLEDGEMENTS

Author: Anna Brett
Editors: Joe Fullman and Kait Eaton
Consultant: Kristina Routh
Illustrators: Steve James and Craig Eaton
Design: Duck Egg Blue Limited
Publisher: Piers Pickard
Editorial Director: Joe Fullman
Art Director: Andy Mansfield
Print Production: Nigel Longuet

Published in September 2022
by Lonely Planet Global Limited
CRN: 554153
ISBN: 978-1-83869-528-6
10 9 8 7 6 5 4 3 2 1

Printed in China

STAY IN TOUCH

lonelyplanet.com/contact

Lonely Planet Office:

IRELAND
Digital Depot, Roe Lane (off Thomas St),
Digital Hub, Dublin 8, D08 TCV4, Ireland

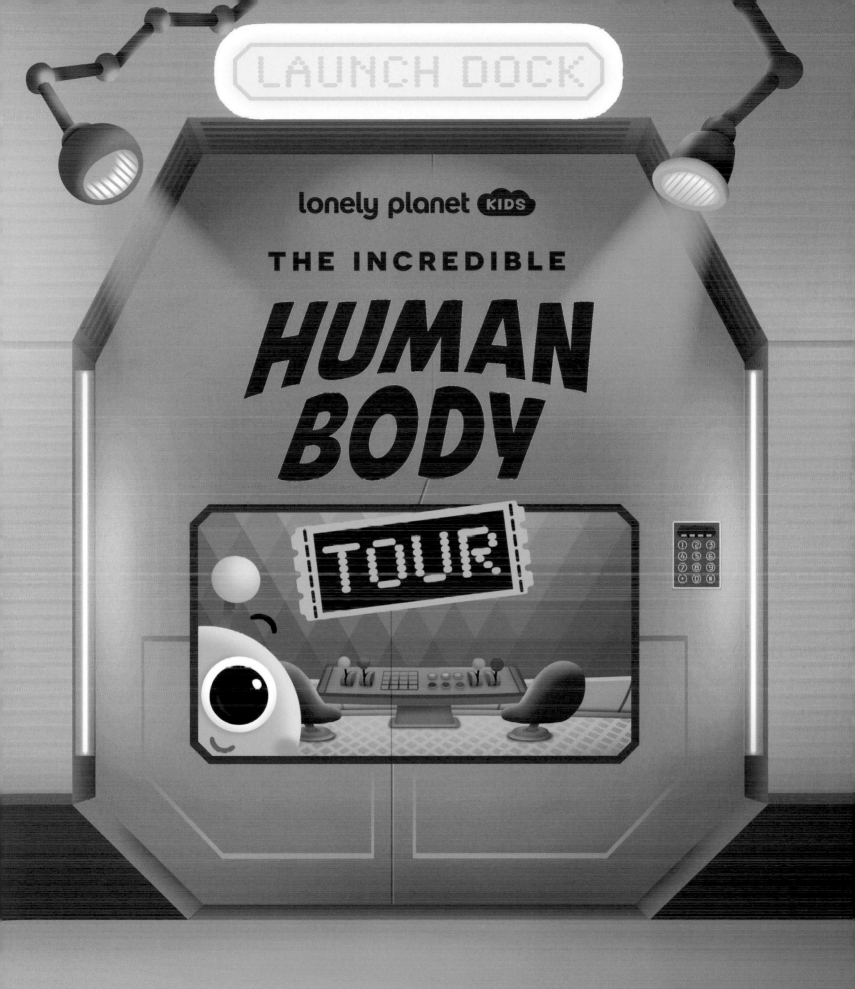

CONTENTS

MEET YOUR GUIDES

Step right up! Join us for a guided tour around the most amazing place in the Universe—the human body. We'll explore the brain, take a peek around the nervous system, check out a skeleton, and discover what it's like to be pumped along blood vessels, squeezed through the intestines, and sneezed out of the nose. It's a trip you'll never forget!

Hello, welcome, and thank you for joining our tour today! I'm Dewlap and my little green friend is Hallux. Together we'll be taking you on a tour of the human body. And we'll be seeing most of it from the INSIDE!

There's so much to see that we'll be traveling by a special vehicle—the Bodyscope Bus. Its technology will enable us to shrink down when we need to, and special cameras on board will enable us to see through **tissue** and **bone** to check out what lies beneath. Most importantly, it will protect us from some of the more hostile areas of the body.

HEY, DON'T FORGET ME! I'M BOT, THE DROID, AND I'M FULL OF FACTS. BECAUSE I'M SMALL I CAN EXPLORE AREAS THE OTHERS CAN'T GET TO!

MULTIFUNCTION ARM

STOMACH **ACID**-PROOF PAINTWORK

LIGHT-SENSITIVE HEADLIGHTS

I'M THE BODYSCOPE BUS AND I'M SPECIALLY DESIGNED FOR THIS KIND OF JOURNEY. HIDDEN AWAY INSIDE I HAVE MAGNIFICATION EQUIPMENT, SAMPLE COLLECTING KITS, HEADPHONES, TAPE MEASURES, SPARE PARTS, AND TABLET SCREENS, SO WE CAN REALLY STUDY THE INNER WORKINGS OF THE BODY.

PROPELLERS FOR FLYING AND SWIMMING

DOOR

IMAGE PROJECTOR/ SEE-THROUGH CAMERA

RETRACTABLE ALL-TERRAIN WHEELS

FACT FLASH_Look for these Fact Flashes for more fascinating info on the body. Plus, you can find the meaning of any special words shown in **bold** in the glossary on page 140.

SENSING THE WORLD

Welcome to the control center! The first stop on our grand tour is the brain—the headquarters of the body. The brain tells the body what to do and is a huge filing cabinet for all the information, memories, and emotions that humans have.

The brain operates 24 hours a day, 7 days a week—even while the body is sleeping. Messages are constantly whizzing backward and forward at over 250 mph (400 kph).

SIGHTS TO SPOT......................

NERVE **CELLS**: THEY MAKE UP THE PATHWAYS THAT THE BRAIN'S MESSAGES TRAVEL ALONG

CEREBRAL CORTEX: THE WRINKLY OUTER SURFACE OF THE BRAIN

VITREOUS HUMOR: THE LIQUID THAT MAKES UP MOST OF THE EYE'S VOLUME, AND IS 99% WATER

FACT FLASH_The brain grows to three times its size in the first year of life, and will continue to grow for 18 years!

BODY MAP

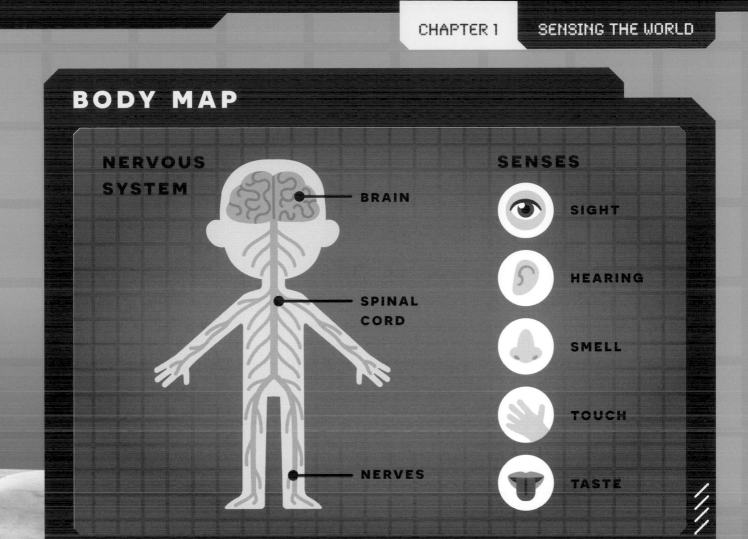

NERVOUS SYSTEM

BRAIN

SPINAL CORD

NERVES

SENSES

SIGHT

HEARING

SMELL

TOUCH

TASTE

As you can see on the Body Map, we'll also be visiting the nervous system and the **senses** in this part of the tour. The nervous system is the network the brain uses to send messages around the body. The senses are sight, hearing, smell, touch, and taste. The nervous system and senses work together to help humans understand the world around them.

THE BRAIN

We need to tread carefully here, as we're currently near the area of the brain responsible for the body's emotions, and we don't want to accidentally trigger a gush of tears! The big pink spongy bit you can see is called the cerebrum and it is responsible for memory, speech, emotions, learning, and conscious actions. There are billions of **nerve** cells in the cerebrum, all working at high speed.

I'VE TURNED ON MY PROJECTOR SO WE CAN SEE THE DIFFERENT PARTS OF THE BRAIN. THE CEREBRUM IS DIVIDED INTO FOUR AREAS, CALLED LOBES, WHICH PROCESS DIFFERENT THOUGHTS AND ACTIONS.

FRONTAL LOBE:
IMPORTANT FOR PLANNING AND THINKING

PARIETAL LOBE:
IMPORTANT FOR SMELL, TASTE, AND TOUCH

TEMPORAL LOBE:
IMPORTANT FOR HEARING AND MEMORY

OCCIPITAL LOBE:
IMPORTANT FOR SIGHT

CEREBRUM

CEREBRUM MAP

The right half of the cerebrum controls the left side of the body, and the right half controls the left side of the body! The right half also helps more with creative activities, like music and art, while the left half of the brain is more logical, helping with reading and math, for example.

**LEFT:
LOGIC**

**RIGHT:
CREATIVITY**

At the bottom of the brain is a long thin structure called the brain stem. It controls **reflexes** and basic bodily functions needed to stay alive, like breathing, digesting, and heart beating. The brain stem connects the rest of the brain to the spinal cord, which is the main pathway of the nervous system.

This small area of the brain is called the cerebellum and it's responsible for movement and balance. It remembers how to do things like walking and running, so these actions feel automatic. Hop, skip, and jump everyone!

CEREBELLUM

BRAIN STEM

MEMORY MATTERS

Wow! Did you see that, Dewlap? I think that was a memory! We are by the hippocampus area of the brain now.

HIPPOCAMPUS

Let's shrink down and take a closer look at what's going on.

NERVE CELL

Nerve cells carry messages from the brain around the body in the form of electrical signals.

These nerve cells are springing into action as the memory reminds the body what to do with candles on a birthday cake.

SYNAPSE

Where two nerve cells meet there is a gap called a synapse. The first cell releases chemicals that travel across the gap and the second cell picks these up and translates them into the original message.

NERVE MAP

NERVE CELLS

MOUTH

NOSE

LUNGS

Using this network of nerve cells, these messages are now traveling at top speed to the nose, lungs, and mouth.

The messages are telling the various body parts what they need to do next.

IT'S TAKEN LESS THAN A SECOND FOR THE MESSAGES TO TRAVEL AROUND THE BODY!

SO, HERE WE GO! TAKE A DEEP BREATH INTO THE LUNGS, LEAN TOWARD THE CAKE, PURSE THE LIPS, AND...

...BLOW...

Once the brain has learned what to do with candles on a cake, it never forgets! Memories and emotions like these are what the **mind** is made of.

NERVOUS SYSTEM

All aboard! It's now time to leave the brain and hit the spinal cord highway. The Bodyscope Bus has around 40 miles (60 km) of nerve pathways to explore in the body's nervous system. The brain links to the spinal cord, which is the central **communications** road for electrical messages to travel along, and together they make up the central nervous system. Nerves then branch out to all the body parts in what's called the peripheral nervous system.

BODY MAP

FULL NERVOUS SYSTEM

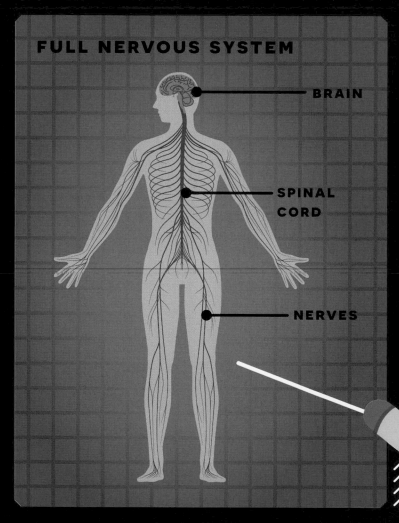

BRAIN

SPINAL CORD

NERVES

Here's a map showing the full nervous system. You can see that nerves cover the entire body, so we can use this network to travel wherever we want to!

SUPER SENSES

THERE ARE FIVE SENSE **ORGANS**, WHICH HAVE **RECEPTOR** NERVE CELLS THAT FEED ELECTRICAL SIGNALS INTO THE NERVOUS SYSTEM.

 RESPONDS TO TOUCH AND TEMPERATURE

SKIN

 RESPONDS TO TASTE

TONGUE

 RESPONDS TO SMELL

NOSE

 RESPONDS TO LIGHT

EYE

 RESPONDS TO SOUND

EAR

The brain tells the body what to do, but it needs to receive information from the outside world to know how to make the body respond. This is where the senses come in —they pass messages from outside of the body to the brain via the nervous system.

THE EYE

Here we are, at sensory stop number one—the eye! Sight is one of the most important ways the body interprets what is happening around it. Here, we're looking inside the eye, where we can see the retina at the back. At the front is the pupil, an opening through which light travels in—and through which the outside world can be seen!

CORNEA

Take a tour around the eye with us! The Bodyscope Bus's projector is explaining what each area of the eye does.

IRIS
THIS IS THE COLORED AREA OF THE EYE AND IT CONTROLS THE SIZE OF THE PUPIL

PUPIL
THIS DARK CIRCLE IS A HOLE IN THE IRIS THAT LETS THROUGH LIGHT

CORNEA
A CLEAR DOME OVER THE EYE THAT BENDS THE LIGHT RAYS AS THEY ENTER

LENS
THIS HELPS THE EYE FOCUS THE LIGHT RAYS ONTO THE BACK OF THE EYE

VITREOUS HUMOR
THE EYEBALL IS FILLED WITH THIS JELLY-LIKE LIQUID

RETINA
THIS IS WHERE THE LIGHT IS FOCUSED SO CELLS CALLED RODS AND CONES CAN INTERPRET IT AND TURN IT INTO AN ELECTRICAL MESSAGE

OPTIC NERVE
THIS IS THE NERVE PATHWAY THAT TAKES THE MESSAGE FROM THE EYE TO THE BRAIN

FACT FLASH_The whole eye is about the size of a ping-pong ball.

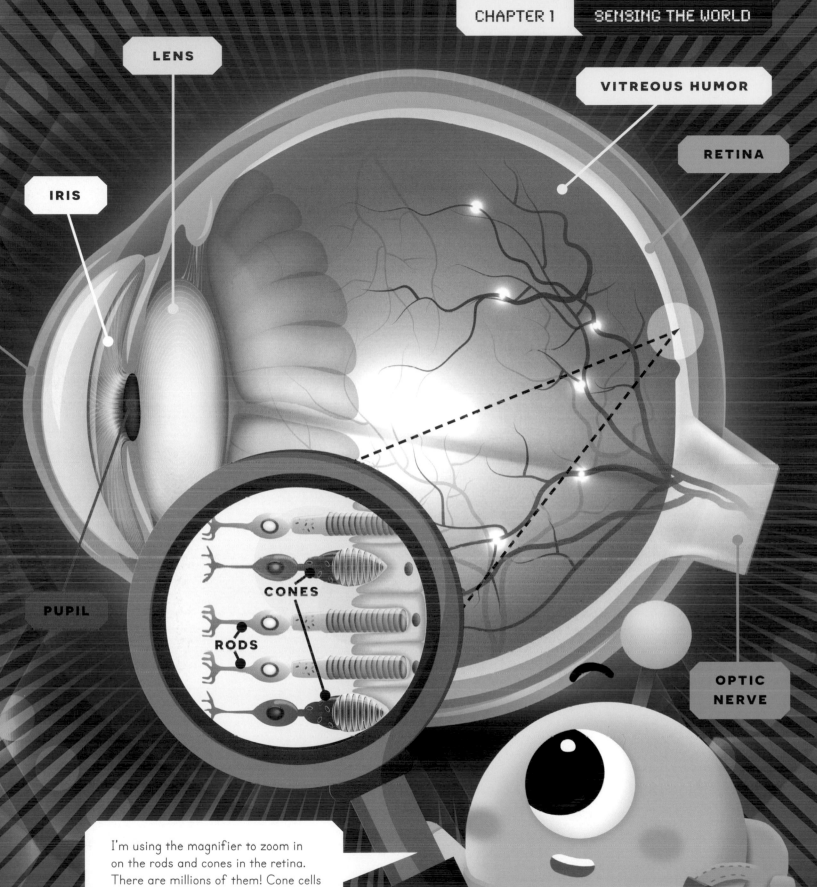

VITREOUS HUMOR

RETINA

LENS

IRIS

PUPIL

CONES

RODS

OPTIC NERVE

I'm using the magnifier to zoom in on the rods and cones in the retina. There are millions of them! Cone cells are able to detect colored and bright light, and rods work in low light.

17

EYE SPY

Sight is a very important sense, and the eye is extremely delicate, so it has to be well-protected. It sits within a gap in the skull called the eye socket, protected by the orbital bone. Six **muscles** hold the eye in place, while also allowing it to move around.

ORBITAL BONE

Each eye sends a slightly different 2D picture to the brain, but the brain is so clever it combines the pictures into one 3D image, from which it can tell how far away an object is.

EYE MUSCLE

EYE MAP

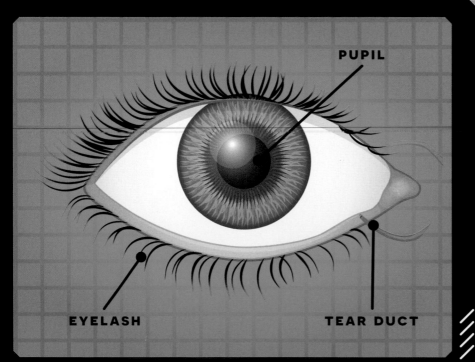

PUPIL

EYELASH

TEAR DUCT

FACT FLASH_ Humans blink more than 10,000 times a day. Blinking is a reflex, so it happens automatically, but the brain can also instruct the eye to do an extra blink if it wants to!

EYE SOCKET

EYELID

Eyelids are folds of skin that open and close over the eye when the brain tells them to blink. Hairs along the edge of each eyelid, called eyelashes, act like flyswatters to keep dirt and unwanted objects out of the eye, and a tiny bit of fluid washes away any dust with each blink. Tear ducts in the bottom corner of the eye drain away the fluid. If the eye gets poked, lots of fluid comes out, the tear ducts overflow, and the extra liquid rolls down the face as tears.

HOLD ON, WE'RE NOT READY TO LEAVE THE BODY JUST YET, HALLUX!

EYELASHES

CATCH!

Let's take a peek through the pupil at what's happening outside, Dewlap. Look, a ball is flying straight toward the body!

Seems like it's time for the eye to show off its supersensory sight skills!

THE EYE

The muscles in the iris get to work and widen (dilate) the pupil so lots of light can rush into the eye. This will help the brain figure out exactly what is going on as quickly as possible.

UNDILATED PUPIL

DILATED PUPIL

I'm confused. The image has been flipped upside down in the jelly-like vitreous humor. Why?

Don't worry, Hallux, this is no problem for the brain—as we'll see shortly. The cornea and the lens have focused the light directly onto the retina at the back of the eye, and now the rod and cone cells are doing their job, translating the brightness and color levels into electrical messages.

Now it's time for the optic nerve to whisk the image to the brain, where it can then tell the body how to respond.

OPTIC NERVE

BRAIN

The brain has received two picture messages, one from each eye. It combines them, flips them the right way up, and makes them 3D. This allows it to understand that the ball is flying straight toward the face, and FAST!

Instructions go to the hands via the nervous system, and they instantly reach up to catch the ball.

The whole process has taken less than a second! Phew!

THE EAR

Listen up everyone, we've now arrived at our next stop—the ear. The main job of the ear is to collect **sound** and pass it to the brain to be processed. Sound travels in waves, and the inside of the ear is perfectly designed to vibrate when these sound waves hit. So don't be alarmed if we start to wobble around a little in this part of the tour!

WARNING: NEVER PUT ANYTHING INSIDE YOUR EARS, AS YOU COULD DAMAGE THE SENSITIVE EARDRUM.

OSSICLES

EAR DRUM

COCHLEA

There are three sections to the ear: the outer ear, the middle ear, and the inner ear. I am currently in the middle ear. This thin piece of tissue, which the Bodyscope Bus has highlighted in blue, is called the eardrum and it works just like a drum! The sound waves collected by the outer ear hit the eardrum and cause it to vibrate, which in turn makes three small bones, collectively called the ossicles, vibrate too.

22

PINNA

EAR CANAL

BE CAREFUL YOU TWO! THE VIBRATIONS IN THE EAR MAY MAKE YOU LOSE YOUR BALANCE AND FALL INTO EARWAX, WHICH IS THERE TO TRAP DIRT AND STOP IT FROM ENTERING THE EAR.

The pinna is the part of the ear we can see on the outside of someone's head. The shape of the pinna helps to funnel sound waves into the ear canal. Together the pinna and ear canal form the outer ear.

FACT FLASH_ The inner ear is where vibrations are picked up by hairs in the cochlea and changed into nerve signals that can travel to the brain.

GOOD VIBRATIONS

There's music playing outside and the waves are coming down the ear canal. Let's follow the sound waves around the inner ear. The eardrum is thumping, and the three small bones are tap, tap, tapping each other.

SEMICIRCULAR CANALS

VESTIBULAR NERVE

COCHLEAR NERVE

I'm watching the cochlea to see what happens next. It is a spiral-shaped **membrane** lined with over 15,000 hairs and filled with fluid. When the stapes bone taps on the outside, the fluid inside moves. This sways the tiny hairs and they send out electrical impulses into the nervous system along the cochlear nerve. The sound has been converted from waves in the air into a signal the brain can understand.

STAPES BONE

NEAR THE COCHLEA ARE THE THREE SEMICIRCULAR CANALS—TUBES OF FLUID THAT HELP THE BODY STAY BALANCED. THE FLUID WITHIN THEM MOVES ACCORDING TO HOW THE HEAD TILTS, AND TINY HAIRS IN THE FLUID SEND MESSAGES TO THE BRAIN. THESE MESSAGES TRAVEL ALONG THE VESTIBULAR NERVE TO THE BRAIN, TELLING IT IF THE BODY IS MOVING FORWARD, BACKWARD, UP, DOWN, OR SIDE TO SIDE.

FACT FLASH_The sounds humans hear are all within a certain frequency range—this means how close sound waves are to each other. Waves close together make high-pitched sounds, like that of a dog whistle.

MALLEUS BONE

INCUS BONE

SOUND WAVES

THE NOSE

We've traveled from the ears to the nose —welcome to the body's third sense! Now, I'm sure you all know that air comes into the body through the nose, but so do **odor molecules**. And this is where the olfactory system, the body's sense of smell, works its magic.

I'VE HIGHLIGHTED THE INSIDE OF THE NASAL CAVITY PURPLE AND MADE ANY BLOOD VESSELS LOOK TRANSPARENT, SO WE CAN CLEARLY SEE WHAT'S GOING ON. WHEN THE BODY BREATHES IN AIR, TINY MOLECULES OF ODOR ALSO ENTER THE NOSE THROUGH THE NOSTRILS. THEY SWIRL AROUND THE NASAL CHAMBER—JUST LIKE HALLUX AND DEWLAP!

OLFACTORY BULB

SMELL RECEPTORS

The smell receptor cells are located in the olfactory bulb. These cells are covered in tiny hairs, made of nerves, which pick up the odor molecules. So when a smell molecule lands on a hair, the nerve sends messages about the smell to the brain.

THE NOSE CAN TELL THE DIFFERENCE BETWEEN BILLIONS OF SMELLS! WHAT'S THIS ONE... A FLOWER?

When the nose sends messages about a smell to the brain, the pathway it uses in the nervous system also connects to the area of the brain that deals with emotions and memories. This is why certain smells might make you remember past events, and bring about an emotional response as to whether a smell is good—or bad!

FACT FLASH_About 80 percent of taste comes from the sense of smell. This explains why it is harder to taste food when the body has a cold and the nose is blocked.

ACHOO!

Whoops! I've just tripped over some hairs and tickled the inside of the nose. We'd better hold on tight, Dewlap—there might be a sneeze coming!

Nose hairs work to trap dust and dirt and stop it entering the nasal passages.

BODY MAP

SNEEZING MUSCLES

- EYELIDS
- THROAT
- CHEST
- DIAPHRAGM
- ABDOMINAL MUSCLES

The brain has been alerted and sends out a message to all the muscles needed to make the nose sneeze. That's the abdominal muscles, chest, diaphragm, throat, eyelids... Phew, it's a complex process!

Here we go! The eyelids are shutting, the muscles in the chest are expanding, and the tongue has moved to the top of the mouth. There goes a deep breath in...

We'd better get our umbrellas up! It's starting to rain **mucus** in the nose now. Mucus is made by cells and is sticky and gloopy so it can trap any unwanted particles in the body and remove them.

Here it comes! Quick everyone, get into the Bodyscope Bus! Air is being forced out of the body and EVERYTHING in the nose must go... Ah, too late!

SALIVA AND MUCUS DROPLETS CAN TRAVEL AT SPEEDS OF UP TO 100 MPH (160 KPH)!

FEEDING AND GROWING

Well, that was a roller-coaster ride! We've been sneezed out of the nose and have ended up in the mouth. Which is handy, as this is the start of the next section of the tour. This is where we'll learn about digestion—the process the body uses to break down food into **nutrients** that it can use for energy, growth, and to repair itself.

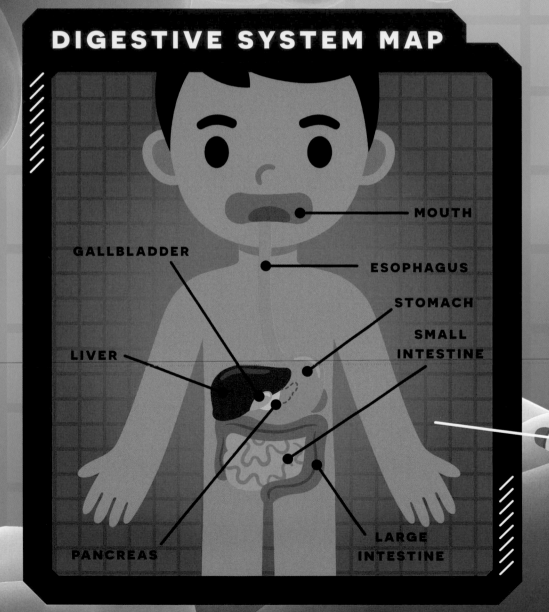

DIGESTIVE SYSTEM MAP

MOUTH

GALLBLADDER

ESOPHAGUS

STOMACH

SMALL INTESTINE

LIVER

PANCREAS

LARGE INTESTINE

Let's plan our route through the digestive system with the help of this map. As you can see, we will start in the mouth, then we'll need to travel down the esophagus and into the stomach, small intestine, and large intestine to see where the real action happens.

SIGHTS TO SPOT....................

HELPFUL BACTERIA: TINY ORGANISMS LIVING IN THE INTESTINE THAT HELP DIGEST FOOD AND PROTECT THE BODY FROM DANGEROUS **INFECTIONS**

ENZYMES: CHEMICALS THAT HELP WITH THE PROCESS OF BREAKING DOWN FOOD INTO SMALL MOLECULES THAT THE BODY CAN ABSORB AND USE

TOOTH

We're currently entering the "cafeteria" area of the body—all food that goes into it enters through the mouth. Here, teeth crush and tear the food, saliva softens it, and the tongue helps move everything around.

TONGUE

THE FULL DIGESTIVE PROCESS CAN TAKE BETWEEN SIX HOURS AND A FEW DAYS.

CRUNCH AND MUNCH

First, let's take a look at things at the front of the mouth, particularly the teeth and tongue. Teeth are hard rigid structures, while the tongue is a long, soft, flexible muscle. They work together to begin the process of breaking down food, so it can be swallowed and digested.

Watch out, Hallux, don't get crushed by those molars! When the mouth is hard at work chewing food, it's the job of the teeth to slice, tear, crunch, and munch anything and everything in their way. This is the first stage of the digestive process.

MOUTH MAP

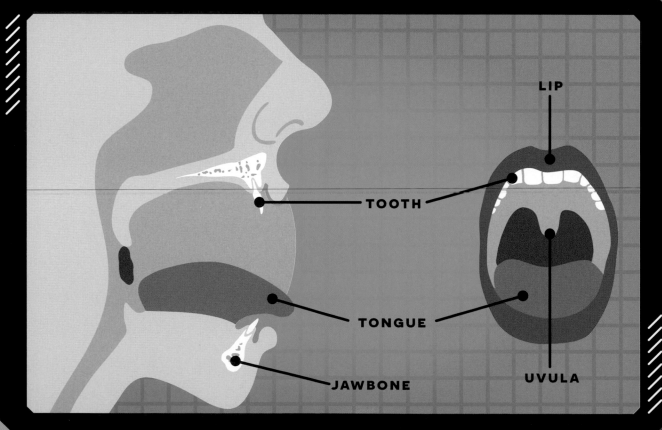

LIP

TOOTH

TONGUE

UVULA

JAWBONE

FACT FLASH_ The mouth is where the sense of taste is. The tongue and **saliva** combine to help the body taste the flavor of the food it eats.

When we flew into the mouth, we passed the lips. These are full of nerves, which means they are very sensitive, but they are also very practical, as they close around the teeth to keep food in the mouth!

THE JAWBONE, OR MANDIBLE, IS THE LARGEST AND STRONGEST BONE IN THE FACE, HOLDING ALL THE LOWER TEETH IN PLACE. MUSCLES SURROUNDING THE JAWBONE MAKE THE MOUTH MOVE UP AND DOWN, ALLOWING THE TEETH TO GET TO WORK.

THE TEETH

We've counted, and there are 32 teeth in the adult mouth. We can see four different types of teeth as well. The body goes through two sets of teeth over a lifetime, but the baby set only consists of 20 teeth and lasts for around six years.

CHECK OUT THE DIFFERENT TYPES OF TEETH WITH THE HELP OF THE PROJECTOR ON THE BODYSCOPE BUS.

INCISORS X 8

THE STRAIGHT, SHARP EDGES ON THESE TEETH MAKE THEM PERFECT TOOLS FOR BITING INTO FOOD.

MOLARS X 12

THESE BIG POWERFUL TEETH CAN BE FOUND AT THE BACK OF THE MOUTH. THEY CRUSH AND GRIND FOOD ACROSS THEIR LARGE BUMPY SURFACE.

FACT FLASH_ Gums are like a soft skin covering the teeth and jawbone. Gums keep the teeth in place and protect them from bacteria.

CANINES X 4

WORKING ALONGSIDE THE INCISORS, THESE POINTED TEETH ARE GREAT AT GRIPPING AND TEARING TOUGHER FOOD.

PRE-MOLARS X 8

SIMILAR TO THE MOLARS IN SHAPE, THESE WIDE TEETH ARE USED FOR CHEWING AND CRUSHING.

Each tooth is covered in hard enamel. Below that is softer dentin, and beneath that is the pulp, where the nerve and blood supply runs deep down into the root of the tooth. It is important to protect the top section of the tooth, called the crown, by brushing. This is to keep the enamel strong—if it gets damaged, tooth decay can happen, which damages the tooth's internal workings.

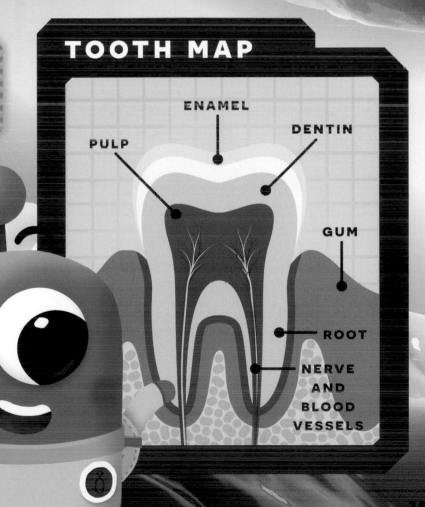

TOOTH MAP

PULP

ENAMEL

DENTIN

GUM

ROOT

NERVE AND BLOOD VESSELS

MIX IT UP

Before the body has even taken a bite of food, it springs into action by filling the mouth with saliva. This is a liquid containing enzymes, which moistens and begins to break down the lumps of food the teeth have taken a bite of. Umbrellas up, here comes another deluge of saliva!

The tongue is a hardworking muscle, about 3 in. (8 cm) in length. It pushes food around the mouth and between the teeth in order to roll it into a ball called a bolus.

Looking closely, we can see the tongue is covered in lots of bumps, called papillae. They help the tongue grip and also contain the taste buds. Taste buds are made of receptor cells, which detect the flavor molecules in food, and nerve cells, which relay the taste information to the brain. They help the body respond to food that tastes good—and bad!

PAPILLA

TASTE BUD

NERVES

THE TONGUE REALLY IS AMAZING! IT'S HOME TO OVER 10,000 TASTE BUDS, WHICH ARE REPLACED EVERY COUPLE OF WEEKS.

ONCE THE FOOD HAS BEEN NICELY CHEWED, THE TONGUE PUSHES IT TOWARD THE BACK OF THE MOUTH AND A REFLEX ACTION CALLED SWALLOWING BEGINS. A FLAP CALLED THE EPIGLOTTIS COVERS THE ENTRANCE TO THE WINDPIPE, MEANING FOOD CAN TRAVEL DOWN THE ESOPHAGUS AND INTO THE STOMACH. LET'S FOLLOW THIS SWALLOW...

BREATHING

SWALLOWING

EPIGLOTTIS UP

AIR FLOWING INTO OPEN TRACHEA (WINDPIPE)

ESOPHAGUS CLOSED

EPIGLOTTIS DOWN

TRACHEA CLOSED

FOOD FLOWING INTO OPEN ESOPHAGUS

GULP IT DOWN

Here we go! The mouth has swallowed the food down into the esophagus—a muscular tube that leads to the stomach. Thankfully, the esophagus isn't a top-and-side tube, so there's no need to worry about us falling down it like a water chute!

THE ESOPHAGUS WORKS TO TRANSPORT FOOD ALONG IT IN A PROCESS CALLED PERISTALSIS, WHICH WORKS LIKE A WAVE. MUSCLES RELAX, ALLOWING FOOD TO MOVE ALONG THE TUBE. THEY THEN SQUEEZE TO PUSH THE FOOD ONWARD AND STOP IT MOVING BACK UP TOWARD THE MOUTH. THIS MEANS FOOD WILL ALWAYS TRAVEL TOWARD THE STOMACH, EVEN IF THE BODY IS UPSIDE DOWN!

Get the tape measure out, Hallux! Did you know the esophagus grows with the body? It is around 3 in. (8 cm) long at birth and around 10 in. (25 cm) long as an adult.

FACT FLASH_ The esophagus is also called the foodpipe or gullet.

ESOPHAGUS MAP

HOW PERISTALSIS WORKS

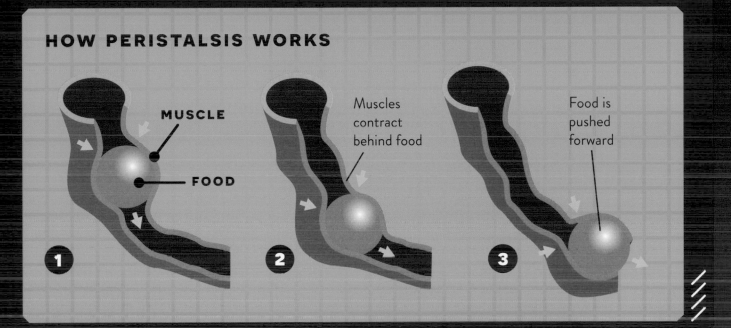

MUSCLE

FOOD

Muscles contract behind food

Food is pushed forward

1

2

3

Of course, sometimes food does travel back up the esophagus—take vomiting for example! When this happens, the body tells the muscles in the esophagus to relax so the stomach can force unwanted food up and out.

SPLASHDOWN!

We've landed in the stomach! This bag of muscle is filled with liquid—stomach acid and enzymes to be precise, which are also known as gastric juices.

Everyone needs to stay inside the Bodyscope Bus—the conditions outside are hazardous! The churning process is about to begin... it's going to be a rocky ride!

LONGITUDINAL LAYER

CIRCULAR LAYER

OBLIQUE LAYER

Hold on tight! The three layers of muscle in the stomach are working hard, contracting and relaxing in order to change the shape of the stomach and move everything inside around.

The three muscle layers are called the oblique layer, the circular layer, and the longitudinal layer.

Uh oh! What's that sound, Hallux?

Don't worry, it's just a stomach rumble! It happens when air mixes with the liquid in the stomach and gurgles.

Woah! We've been pushed up against the stomach wall! Look how it is lined with lots of little holes called gastric pits. These are tiny openings through which the acid and digestive **enzymes** are released into the stomach by **glands**.

GASTRIC PIT

The gastric juices then help break down the food in the stomach. The liquid is so acidic it can dissolve steel—thankfully the Bodyscope Bus has a tough outer shell!

Let's scoop up some liquid for analysis.

The liquid food mush that sits in the stomach once the gastric juices have done their work is called chyme. Muscles push the chyme to the end of the stomach, where it exits through a sphincter muscle and continues its digestive journey. A sphincter is a circle of muscle that opens to let things pass and closes to keep them in.

SPHINCTER MUSCLE

CHYME

THE STOMACH

The stomach can be found in the upper left area of the body's abdomen. Its size varies depending on the person—and how much they eat! Folds in the stomach wall open out and allow it to stretch to hold a big meal. Even though its contents are highly acidic, the stomach itself remains undamaged because cells along its lining ooze a layer of protective mucus.

The map below will help you familiarize yourself with the stomach's main areas.

STOMACH MAP

There are sphincter muscles at the entrance and exit points of the stomach to keep food inside until it is ready to pass through.

FUNDUS
The curved area at the top of the stomach, near the entrance

CARDIA
The area where the esophagus joins the stomach

BODY
The main area of the stomach

PYLORUS
A narrow section where the stomach joins the small intestine

ANTRUM
The lowest part of the stomach

DIGESTIVE HELPERS

ONCE ACID IN THE STOMACH HAS BROKEN DOWN THE FOOD, ENZYMES IN THE SMALL INTESTINE SPLIT IT UP INTO MOLECULES THE BODY CAN USE, LIKE **GLUCOSE** AND FRUCTOSE, WHICH ARE TYPES OF SUGARS.

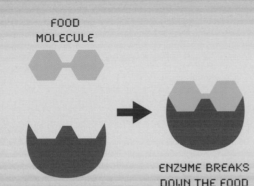

FOOD MOLECULE

GLUCOSE   FRUCTOSE

ENZYME MOLECULE

ENZYME BREAKS DOWN THE FOOD

ENZYME RELEASES MOLECULES INTO BODY

CARBOHYDRATES BREAK DOWN FASTEST IN THE DIGESTIVE SYSTEM. PROTEINS TAKE LONGER AND FATS THE LONGEST OF ALL. BUT WATER PRETTY MUCH PASSES STRAIGHT THROUGH.

FOLD

BACTERIA CAN ENTER THE BODY HIDDEN IN FOOD, BUT STOMACH ACID HELPS KILL OFF THESE UNWANTED GERMS.

FACT FLASH_ Around 6–8 pints (3–4 liters) of gastric juice are made each day—that's more than the typical amount of fluid that goes into the body!

THE SMALL INTESTINE

The Bodyscope Bus is showing us a projection of the next area on our tour, the (not-so-small) small intestine, which consist of around 33 ft. (7 m) of narrow coiled tube. Most of the absorption in the digestive process takes place here. There's plenty of time to look around, as food tends to stay in the small intestine for up to six hours!

THE FIRST SECTION OF THE SMALL INTESTINE IS CALLED THE DUODENUM, WHICH IS ONLY AROUND 12 IN. (30 CM) LONG. HERE, GLANDS RELEASE LIQUID TO FURTHER HELP DIGESTION, ALLOWING THE BODY TO ABSORB ALL THE NUTRIENTS IT NEEDS. IT ALSO WORKS TO NEUTRALIZE THE ACIDS COMING IN FROM THE STOMACH.

THE SMALL INTESTINE IS DIVIDED INTO THREE SECTIONS: THE DUODENUM, THE JEJUNUM, AND THE ILEUM. JUST LIKE WE SAW IN THE ESOPHAGUS, THE SMALL INTESTINE MOVES FOOD ALONG BY PERISTALSIS—MUSCLES SQUEEZING AND RELAXING IN WAVES ALONG THE TUBE.

LARGE INTESTINE

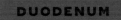

DUODENUM

STOMACH

JEJUNUM

The jejunum makes up most of the small intestine, and is where the villi get to work. Villi are teeny finger-like bumps whose outer walls are just one cell thick, so nutrients can pass through them into a network of blood **capillaries**, where they are taken around the body.

ILEUM

The final section of the small intestine is called the ileum. Most nutrients have been absorbed by the time food gets here, but what's left in this watery liquid now leaves the small intestine and heads into the large intestine to continue its journey.

ABSORPTION

We've seen how food gets down into the small intestine, but how does it actually pass through the digestive system and into the body, we hear you ask. Dewlap and Hallux have ventured into the small intestine to find out. It all happens in a process called absorption, in which strange, worm-like structures called villi have the starring role.

Here, lining the walls of the small intestine, are the villi, the things that do the actual absorbing. Each villus is tiny, just 0.04 in. (1 mm) long. Villi are shaped like fingers, giving them a large surface area, so there's lots of space for nutrients to be absorbed. When digested food molecules reach the villi, they pass through the thin cell walls by diffusion —a bit like a sponge soaking up water.

VILLUS MAP

In this diagram, you can see what the inside of a villus looks like. The blood capillaries transport nutrients around the body. A structure called the lacteal passes other molecules into the lymph fluid (pages 102–103), which we'll learn more about later.

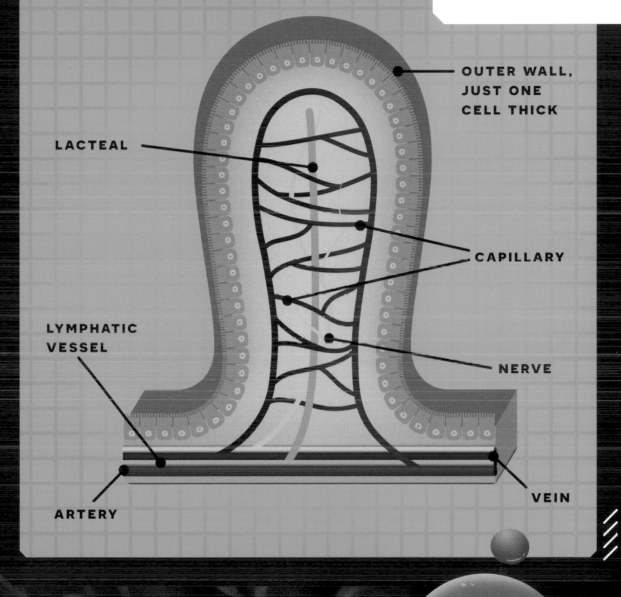

OUTER WALL, JUST ONE CELL THICK

LACTEAL

CAPILLARY

LYMPHATIC VESSEL

NERVE

ARTERY

VEIN

HALLUX AND DEWLAP, MAKE SURE YOU DON'T GET ABSORBED AS WELL! WE'VE GOT MORE OF THE DIGESTIVE SYSTEM TO SEE BEFORE WE START TRAVELING AROUND THE BLOODSTREAM!

OVER AND OUT

It's not a glamorous part of the body, but this is where the undigested leftovers from a meal end up! The large intestine is wider than the small intestine, but not as long—around 6 ft. (2 m) in length. Any remaining water is absorbed here, plus a few **vitamins**. But the rest is then classed as a waste product, turned into feces (poop!), and moved into the rectum.

Look here, Dewlap, I think I've found some friends! These teeny-tiny little creatures are bacteria, and there are around 1,000 different types living in the large intestine. They are only made up of just one cell, but they are able to break down any remaining food.

BACTERIA

With most of the water taken up into the body and helpful bacteria processing the unwanted solids, the chyme originally made by the stomach has now become feces. It sits in the rectum, a tube around 5 in. (12 cm) in length, until it is ready to be pushed out of the body via the anus.

LARGE INTESTINE MAP

BACTERIA IN THE LARGE INTESTINE MAKE GAS AS WELL—THE AMOUNT DEPENDS ON WHAT TYPE OF FOOD AND DRINK HAS ENTERED THE BODY.

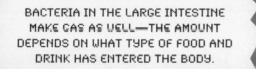

STOMACH

LARGE INTESTINE

RECTUM

ANUS

Gas is expelled from the body

THE LIVER

Welcome to the hardworking liver, a great friend of the digestive system! It is located just above the stomach and does many jobs, including processing and storing some of the nutrients absorbed by the digestive system. It also produces bile, which breaks down fats and neutralizes stomach acid.

Hallux, I've got a glucose snack bar for you! Glucose is an important source of energy for the body—and us tour guides, as we need lots of energy! In the body, the liver is responsible for both storing and making this glucose from nutrients found in things like bread and potatoes. It then releases glucose into the bloodstream when it's needed, like between meals.

LIVER

LOOK! BENEATH THE LIVER IS THE GALLBLADDER. THIS IS WHERE THE LIVER STORES THE BILE IT MAKES. THE GALLBLADDER RELEASES THE BILE INTO THE SMALL INTESTINE, WHERE IT WORKS ITS MAGIC, BREAKING DOWN AND ABSORBING FATS FROM FOOD.

GALL BLADDER

PANCREAS

FACT FLASH_ Weighing over 3 lb. (1 kg), the liver is the second-largest organ in the body (the skin is actually the largest organ).

The liver is also the main defensive help for the intestines. It produces substances that destroy nasty bacteria and it also helps to clean the blood.

SPLEEN

BESIDE THE STOMACH IS THE SPLEEN, AN ORGAN THAT FILTERS BLOOD. AND IF YOU LOOK BENEATH THE STOMACH, YOU'LL SEE THE PANCREAS. THAT'S THE PLACE WHERE ENZYMES RELEASED INTO THE DIGESTIVE SYSTEM ARE MADE.

STOMACH

FOOD FOR FUEL

...automatically, thanks
to the brain sending out
messages all day every
day. But the body can only
carry out the instructions
if it has an energy supply
to help it move, grow,
and think. Just like the
Bodyscope Bus, it needs
fuel to run!

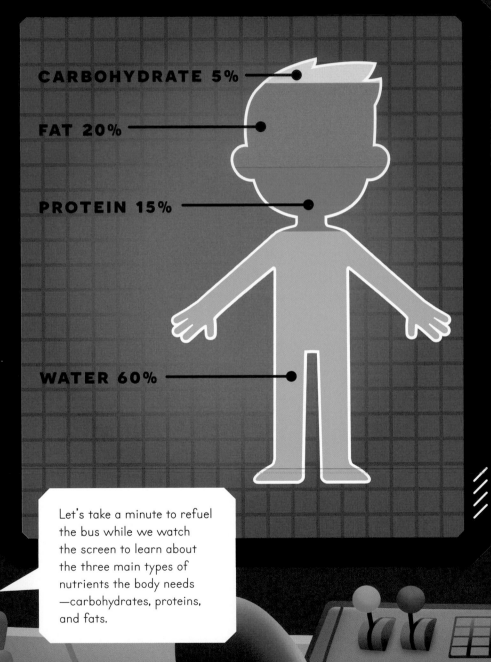

BODY SCAN

CARBOHYDRATE 5%

FAT 20%

PROTEIN 15%

WATER 60%

Let's take a minute to refuel
the bus while we watch
the screen to learn about
the three main types of
nutrients the body needs
—carbohydrates, proteins,
and fats.

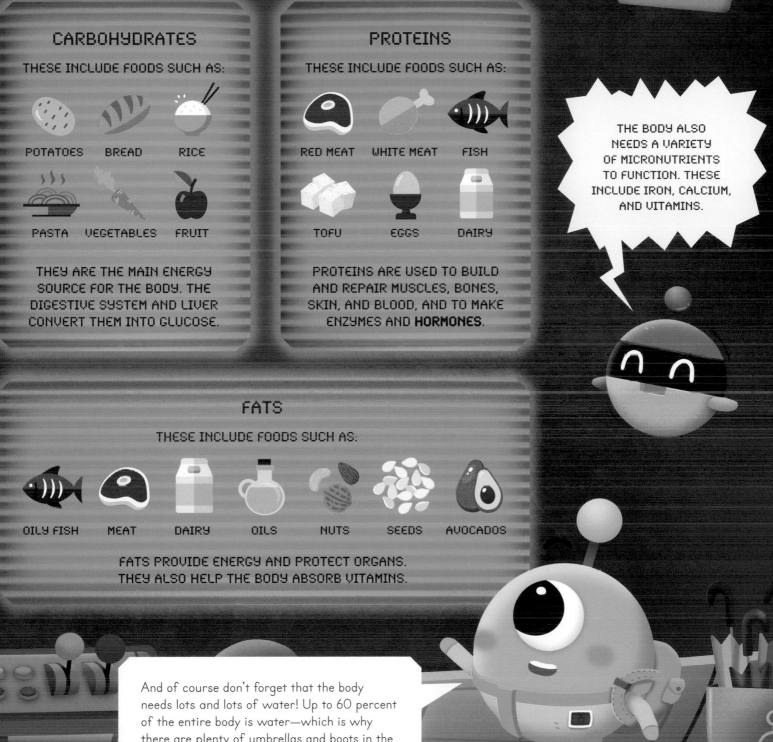

CARBOHYDRATES

THESE INCLUDE FOODS SUCH AS:

POTATOES   BREAD   RICE

PASTA   VEGETABLES   FRUIT

THEY ARE THE MAIN ENERGY SOURCE FOR THE BODY. THE DIGESTIVE SYSTEM AND LIVER CONVERT THEM INTO GLUCOSE.

PROTEINS

THESE INCLUDE FOODS SUCH AS:

RED MEAT   WHITE MEAT   FISH

TOFU   EGGS   DAIRY

PROTEINS ARE USED TO BUILD AND REPAIR MUSCLES, BONES, SKIN, AND BLOOD, AND TO MAKE ENZYMES AND **HORMONES**.

THE BODY ALSO NEEDS A VARIETY OF MICRONUTRIENTS TO FUNCTION. THESE INCLUDE IRON, CALCIUM, AND VITAMINS.

FATS

THESE INCLUDE FOODS SUCH AS:

OILY FISH   MEAT   DAIRY   OILS   NUTS   SEEDS   AVOCADOS

FATS PROVIDE ENERGY AND PROTECT ORGANS. THEY ALSO HELP THE BODY ABSORB VITAMINS.

And of course don't forget that the body needs lots and lots of water! Up to 60 percent of the entire body is water—which is why there are plenty of umbrellas and boots in the Bodyscope Bus for us to use at any time!

While we are having our refueling stop, the body is also taking in some more food. But sometimes after eating, there's too much sugary glucose in the blood, which can have serious health effects for the body.

It's happened, Hallux—the warning systems have been activated. We've traveled into a blood vessel near the pancreas, where we can see there are too many sugar molecules. The body will now call on the help of the pancreas and the super-hormone, insulin, to reduce this sugar high!

WHEN THERE ARE HIGH LEVELS OF GLUCOSE IN THE BLOOD, SPECIAL CELLS IN THE PANCREAS PRODUCE MORE INSULIN. HERE IT IS, FLOODING INTO THE BLOODSTREAM.

INSULIN MOLECULE

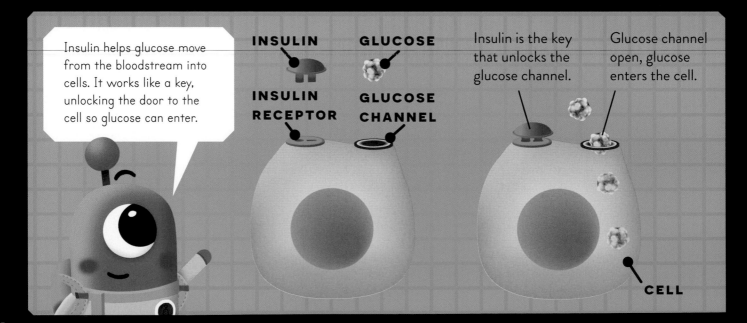

Insulin helps glucose move from the bloodstream into cells. It works like a key, unlocking the door to the cell so glucose can enter.

INSULIN

GLUCOSE

INSULIN RECEPTOR

GLUCOSE CHANNEL

Insulin is the key that unlocks the glucose channel.

Glucose channel open, glucose enters the cell.

CELL

Phew, there's now less glucose in the blood and the body is happy again. Crisis averted!

While all this was happening, the liver has also been hard at work. The glucose it received from the blood has been converted into glycogen and stored away for later.

When the opposite happens, and there's too little glucose in the blood, the pancreas releases the hormone glucagon. This instructs the liver to turn the glycogen back into glucose and release it into the bloodstream.

PANCREAS

GLUCAGON

LIVER

GLUCOSE

BLOOD VESSEL

LIFE SUPPORT

Welcome to the third part of the tour. Here, we'll meet some of the body's ... ... work nonstop every single day. The heart, lungs, muscles, and bones make up the life-support team for the body—they hold it up and keep it working. There's lots to see, so let's try!

CHECK OUT THE BODY SCAN TO SEE THE FOUR DIFFERENT **BODY SYSTEMS** WE'LL BE EXPLORING IN THIS PART OF THE TOUR.

SIGHTS TO SPOT..................

FEMUR: THE LONGEST BONE IN THE BODY (IN THE THIGH)

GLUTEUS MAXIMUS: THE BIGGEST MUSCLE IN THE BODY (IN THE BOTTOM)

RED BLOOD CELLS: THEY ARE ALMOST EVERYWHERE!

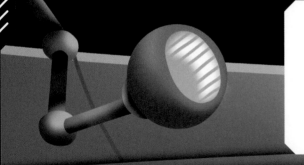

Everyone needs a friend—and I'm lucky to have Hallux by my side! In the body, the heart and lungs are best friends, and the muscles and bones are inseparable buddies. Both pairs work together to help the body, just as Hallux and I work together to be the best tour guides around!

BODY SYSTEMS

CIRCULATORY SYSTEM

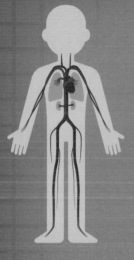

The heart is at the center of the circulatory system; it works with the blood vessels to pump blood all around the body.

RESPIRATORY SYSTEM

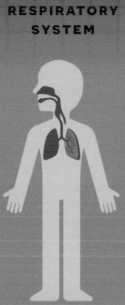

The lungs and airways make up the respiratory system; they carry air into, around, and out of the body.

MUSCULAR SYSTEM

Muscles make up the muscular system; they work every time the body moves—and some even work when the body isn't moving!

SKELETAL SYSTEM

Bones form the skeletal system; this is the framework that holds up the body and gives it its shape.

FACT FLASH_The body has one heart, two lungs, 206 bones, and over 600 muscles.

Look, Dewlap, there's the heart! Let's venture closer to find out more...

THE HEART

SUPERIOR VENA CAVA

Here it is in all its glory... Ladies and gentlemen, this is the heart! This powerful pump beats every second of every day and never gets tired. Made of muscle, the heart moves blood around the body via the blood vessels. The largest blood vessel in the body, the aorta, is the main **artery** taking blood out of the heart to the rest of the body.

RIGHT ATRIUM

Let's take a look around this mighty muscle. As you can see, it's split into a right side and a left side by the septum. Blood flows into the heart from the rest of body and fills a chamber called the right atrium. It then flows into another chamber called the right ventricle.

TRICUSPID VALVE

I'M IN THE RIGHT VENTRICLE. ABOVE ME IS A VALVE CALLED THE TRICUSPID VALVE, WHICH STOPS BLOOD FROM FLOWING THE WRONG WAY. IT'S A BIT LIKE A SIGNPOST FOR US TOUR GUIDES—THERE'S ONLY ONE WAY TO TRAVEL AROUND THE HEART... AND IT'S IN THIS DIRECTION!

RIGHT VENTRICLE

FACT FLASH_The heart is made of a special type of muscle called cardiac muscle, which is only found in this part of the body. See pages 72–73 to find out about other muscle types.

AORTA

PULMONARY ARTERY

PULMONARY VEIN

LEFT ATRIUM

MITRAL VALVE

SEPTUM

LEFT VENTRICLE

ONCE IT'S BEEN THROUGH THE RIGHT VENTRICLE, BLOOD IS PUMPED OUT OF THE HEART VIA THE PULMONARY ARTERIES TO COLLECT **OXYGEN** FROM THE LUNGS. IT THEN RETURNS TO THE HEART VIA THE PULMONARY **VEINS**, FLOWING INTO THE LEFT ATRIUM FIRST, THEN INTO THE LEFT VENTRICLE. THIS OXYGENATED BLOOD THEN LEAVES THE HEART VIA THE AORTA AND IS TRANSPORTED ALL THE WAY AROUND THE BODY AND BACK AGAIN.

The heart beats around 70 times a minute when the body is resting—even more when it's exercising. Each heartbeat is actually two pumps—the first pump sends blood to the lungs and back, and the second pump sends it around the body.

Ready to ride a heartbeat, Dewlap? We've splashed into the blood flowing into the heart from the superior vena cava vein. If we each grab onto a red blood **cell**, we'll be able to ride them through the heart and lungs!

When blood first enters the heart, it fills the right atrium. But there's no time to catch our breath; here comes a squeeze from the muscular walls! The valve at the bottom has opened and—whoosh—we're immediately heading down into the right ventricle!

Whoo! That was fun. Come on, Dewlap, follow me!

Ooh, there's another squeeze of the heart muscles... Did you feel it, Hallux?

Yes, I did. We're up and out through the pulmonary artery and off to the lungs now.

Here we are at the lungs, but there's no time to look around. Those white things are molecules of oxygen flooding into the bloodstream from the alveoli (pages 70–71) and being picked up by the red blood cells.

There's oxygen in all of these red blood cells now.

Ride that wave, Hallux! We're surfing the oxygenated blood back through the pulmonary vein into the heart, through the left atrium, and into the left ventricle.

Hold on tight and get ready for a big one! We are now surrounded by the strongest muscles in the heart. With the next beat we will be whisked out through the aorta and around the rest of the body... Goodbye, heart!

BLOOD

Blood is the way the body transports oxygen and nutrients around itself. Blood also picks up waste materials that need to be removed and drops them where they can exit the body. And it's also very helpful in fighting off infections! It does so much that it's no surprise to learn that blood is actually made up of four things: red blood cells, white blood cells, plasma, and platelets. Let's have a look at them all in detail...

Red blood cells are responsible for carrying oxygen to all the other cells in the body. They are flat disks with a slight indent in the center and they get their bright red color from the hemoglobin inside them that collects oxygen from the lungs. Red blood cells live for around four months but, just like platelets, new ones are being made all the time in the bone marrow (pages 84–85).

PLATELETS ARE TINY CELLS THAT HELP BLOOD TO CLOT. IF A BLOOD VESSEL BREAKS AND BLOOD STARTS LEAKING OUT, PLATELETS QUICKLY RUSH TO THE AREA AND BUILD A BARRIER TO CLOSE THE HOLE. PLATELETS ARE MADE IN THE BONE MARROW, WHICH CAN BE FOUND INSIDE BONES, AND THEY LIVE FOR AROUND NINE DAYS.

PLATELETS

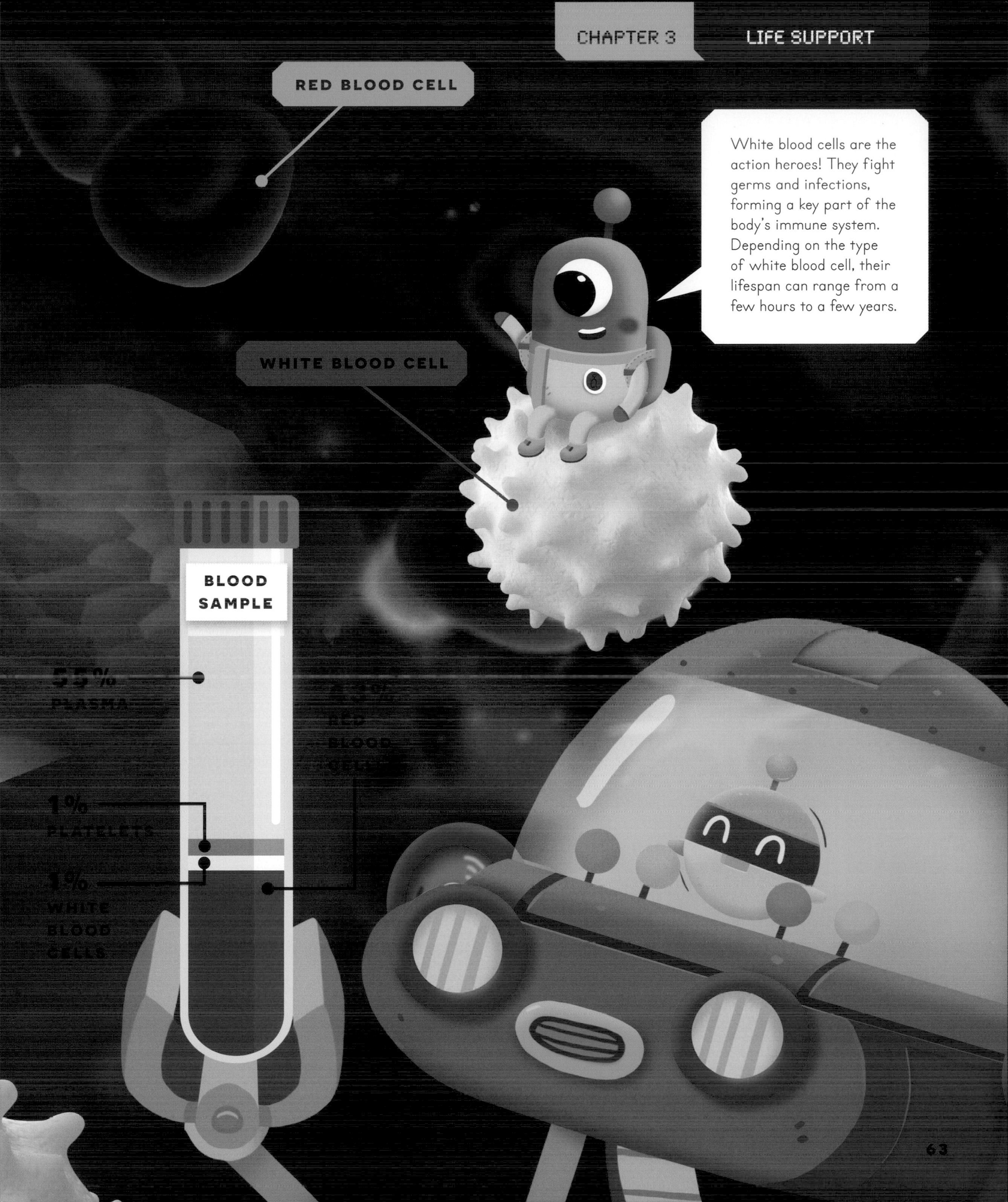
RED BLOOD CELL
White blood cells are the action heroes! They fight germs and infections, forming a key part of the body's immune system. Depending on the type of white blood cell, their lifespan can range from a few hours to a few years.
WHITE BLOOD CELL
BLOOD SAMPLE
55% PLASMA
RED
BLOOD
1% PLATELETS
1% WHITE BLOOD CELLS

CIRCULATION

We now know that the heart pumps the blood around the body, but how does the blood actually get to where it's going? If we look at the Bodyscope Bus's projector, we can see that blood travels along things called blood vessels, and that there are three different types: arteries, veins, and capillaries.

Arteries carry oxygenated blood out of the heart and around the body. The heart is such a powerful pump that blood travels through the arteries at high speed—it takes less than 60 seconds to get around the entire body! The walls of the arteries are thick and elastic so they can withstand the pressure of this super-powerful flow of blood.

ARTERIES AND VEINS

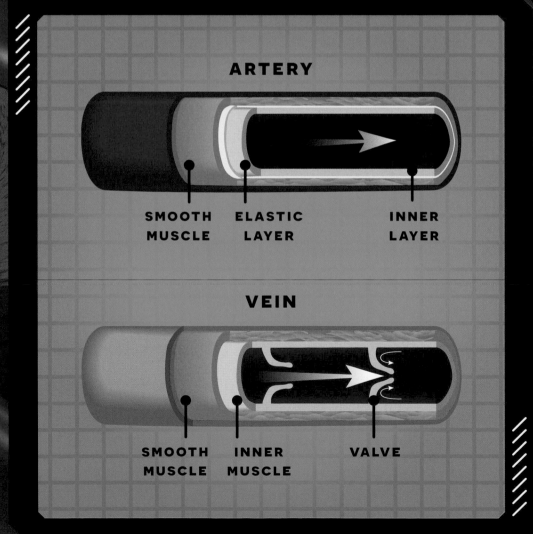

ARTERY

SMOOTH MUSCLE   ELASTIC LAYER   INNER LAYER

VEIN

SMOOTH MUSCLE   INNER MUSCLE   VALVE

ARTERY

CAPILLARIES ARE TINY THIN BLOOD VESSELS THAT BRANCH OUT BETWEEN ARTERIES AND VEINS AND GO INTO EVERY TISSUE IN THE BODY. THEY ALLOW OXYGEN AND OTHER SUBSTANCES IN THE BLOOD TO MOVE ACROSS TO THE CELLS. THEY ALSO PICK UP AND TAKE AWAY WASTE PRODUCTS FROM THE CELLS, SUCH AS **CARBON DIOXIDE**.

Once the blood has finished delivering oxygen around the body, veins carry the deoxygenated blood back to the heart. The blood in veins is lower in pressure than the blood in arteries, so the walls are thinner and less elastic. Veins have valves that only open in one direction, to stop the blood flowing backward.

VEIN

CIRCULATORY SYSTEM

ARTERIES (RED) CONTAIN OXYGENATED BLOOD

HEART

VEINS (BLUE) CONTAIN DEOXYGENATED BLOOD

CAPILLARIES

FACT FLASH_If you laid all of the body's blood vessels end to end, they would stretch over 25,000 miles (40,000 km) —enough to wrap around the world twice!

THE LUNGS

After a short ride along the pulmonary artery, we've reached our next stop—the lungs. Let's look around. With every breath the body takes, air fills the lungs, so it can get a little breezy in here! The role of the lungs is to inhale oxygen and pass it into the blood, so it can be transported around the body for every cell to use. The lungs also remove carbon dioxide by exhaling it out of the body.

We'll try not to get lost in the lungs! There may only be two of them, but within each lung are millions of airways—tubes that get smaller and thinner, like the branches on a tree. The airways cover a huge surface area so air can flow into every inch of space available.

RIGHT LUNG

66

TRACHEA (WINDPIPE)

BRONCHIOLES

BRONCHI

LEFT LUNG

WE CAN CONFIRM THAT THE RIGHT LUNG IS SLIGHTLY WIDER AND SHORTER THAN THE LEFT! THE RIGHT LUNG HAS TO MAKE ROOM FOR THE LIVER BENEATH IT, AND THE LEFT LUNG KINDLY MAKES SPACE FOR THE HEART.

ALVEOLI

At the bottom of the windpipe there's the option to turn left or right into either the left bronchus or the right bronchus—together, these tubes are known as bronchi. The bronchi branch off into thinner tubes called bronchioles, which lead to even smaller, grape-like structures called alveoli, which allow oxygen to pass into the blood through the capillaries surrounding them.

BREATHING

WINDPIPE

The lungs are always busy breathing in and out. They do it every couple of seconds, all day, every day! Most of the time, it happens automatically, but the body can control its breathing if it needs to take a deep breath or blow on something.

The lungs are linked to the mouth by the windpipe, or trachea. This is a tube made of rings of **cartilage**. These rings keep the windpipe rigid and open so air can freely flow up and down it.

IF AIR TRAVELS IN THROUGH THE NOSE, IT IS WARMED AND CLEANED BY THE HAIRS INSIDE. BUT IF AIR ENTERS VIA THE MOUTH, THE WINDPIPE IS THERE TO HELP CLEAN IT. STICKY MUCUS TRAPS ANY GERMS, AND TINY CILIA HAIRS MOVE THE MUCUS TO THE THROAT, WHERE IT CAN BE SWALLOWED.

DIAPHRAGM

Breathing requires the use of muscles around the ribs, as well as the special muscle I'm standing on right now. Known as the diaphragm, this arch-shaped layer of muscle moves rhythmically up and down, up and down, up and down... all day long.

FACT FLASH_ The average person breathes in 9 pints (6 liters) of air a minute—that's over 13,000 pints (8,500 liters) a day.

RESPIRATORY SYSTEM

THE BRAIN CONTROLS HOW FAST THE LUNGS BRING IN AIR. IF THE BODY IS EXERCISING, CELLS NEED MORE FUEL, SO THE LUNGS WORK FASTER TO GET MORE OXYGEN INTO THE BODY AND DELIVERED TO THEM.

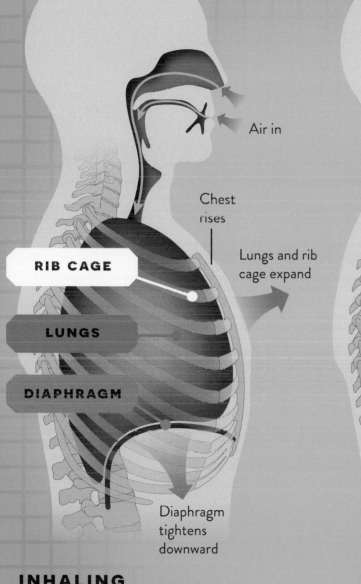

Air in

Chest rises

Lungs and rib cage expand

RIB CAGE

LUNGS

DIAPHRAGM

Diaphragm tightens downward

Air out

Chest falls

Lungs and rib cage shrink

Diaphragm relaxes upward

INHALING

To breathe in, the diaphragm tightens and pulls down, allowing the lungs to expand. At the same time, the ribs move up and out to increase the space for the lungs and allow more air to be sucked into them through the nose and mouth.

EXHALING

To breathe out, the diaphragm muscle relaxes, pushing the lungs back up. The rib cage shrinks back down, which squashes the lungs and forces air up and out through the nose and mouth.

GAS EXCHANGE

OK team, it's time to shrink down and follow a breath of air into the maze of airways that make up the lungs. Eventually, the air ends up at tiny structures known as alveoli, at the end of the bronchioles. This is where the most vital part of breathing happens —a process known as gas exchange— where the body takes in oxygen and gets rid of carbon dioxide.

Alveoli are little air sacs covered in capillary blood vessels. Each alveolus is tiny —about 0.008 in. (0.2 mm) in diameter—and there are millions of them, which give the lungs a huge surface area.

CAPILLARY

Here, you can see gas exchange occurring, as the body takes in oxygen and releases carbon dioxide. Our friendly droid, Bot, will show exactly what's happening over on the screen.

GAS EXCHANGE

CAPILLARY WALL

ALVEOLAR WALL

OXYGEN

CARBON DIOXIDE

RED BLOOD CELLS

Oxygen enters bloodstream

Carbon dioxide leaves bloodstream

OXYGEN MOLECULES FROM THE AIR IN THE LUNGS PASS THROUGH THE WALLS OF THE ALVEOLI AND INTO THE BLOOD IN THE CAPILLARIES SURROUNDING THEM. AT THE SAME TIME, WASTE CARBON DIOXIDE MOLECULES MOVE IN THE OPPOSITE DIRECTION. THEY ENTER THE LUNGS AND ARE EXPELLED FROM THE BODY WHEN WE BREATHE OUT.

FACT FLASH_Oxygen and carbon dioxide move by a process called diffusion. This is where one substance gradually spreads through another, like how paint on a paintbrush colors water in a jar when you swish the brush to clean it.

MUSCLES

Now that the blood is full of oxygen after our visit to the lungs, let's see where this oxygen is used. It's time to explore the muscles, which keep the heart beating, the lungs breathing, and the body moving! Muscles need fuel to work, so they use oxygen to break down the glucose inside cells and turn it into energy.

> Muscles work as a team throughout the body, moving the skeleton around as well as keeping the body alive by pumping the heart. Together, they form the muscular system.

BODY MAP

MUSCLE GROUPS

THE HEAD AND NECK

THE UPPER EXTREMITIES

THE TRUNK

THE LOWER EXTREMITIES

CARDIAC MUSCLE

THIS TYPE OF MUSCLE IS FOUND ONLY IN THE HEART. IT CONTRACTS AND RELAXES AUTOMATICALLY AND NEVER GETS TIRED!

> Here, we can see the skeletal muscles, which are divided into four main muscle groupings: head and neck; the trunk; the upper extremities; and the lower extremities.

FACT FLASH_ There are around 600 muscles in the body. The smallest is the stapedius, which is connected to the smallest bone in the body, the stapes, in the ear (pages 24–25).

THERE ARE THREE TYPES OF MUSCLES: CARDIAC MUSCLE, SMOOTH MUSCLE, AND SKELETAL MUSCLE. THE CELLS ARE ARRANGED DIFFERENTLY IN EACH, AS WE CAN SEE IN THE THREE CLOSE-UPS.

SKELETAL MUSCLE

THESE **MUSCLE FIBERS** ARE ATTACHED TO BONES AND HELP THE BODY TO MOVE. THEY ARE GROUPED INTO PAIRS SO WHEN ONE CONTRACTS, THE OTHER RELAXES. THE BRAIN HAS TO CONSCIOUSLY TELL THESE MUSCLES TO MOVE.

SMOOTH MUSCLE

THIS MUSCLE TYPE IS FOUND IN LAYERS IN THE INTERNAL ORGANS, SUCH AS THE DIGESTIVE SYSTEM AND ARTERIES. IT CONTRACTS IN WAVES, SO IT CAN MOVE FOOD OR BLOOD ALONG IN ONE DIRECTION. JUST LIKE CARDIAC MUSCLE, IT WORKS AUTOMATICALLY.

73

CONTRACT AND RELAX

Time to get up close and personal with a muscle! Muscles are made of fibers, which are small and elastic so they can contract and relax. When they contract and pull, they get shorter. This is what creates the squeeze in the heart muscle, the flex of a biceps, and the constriction of the tubes in the intestines to move food along. But muscles can only pull and then relax, they can't push.

I'm sitting on the deltoid (also known as the shoulder muscle), just above the biceps muscle at the top of the arm.

MUSCLE FIBER

FASCICLE

MYOFIBRIL

MUSCLE

Muscles are made of thin rods called myofibrils. These rods are grouped together to form a muscle fiber. Muscle fibers are grouped together in a larger structure called a fascicle. And fascicles are bundled together in their thousands and wrapped in a thin membrane to make up the whole muscle.

MYOFIBRIL MAP

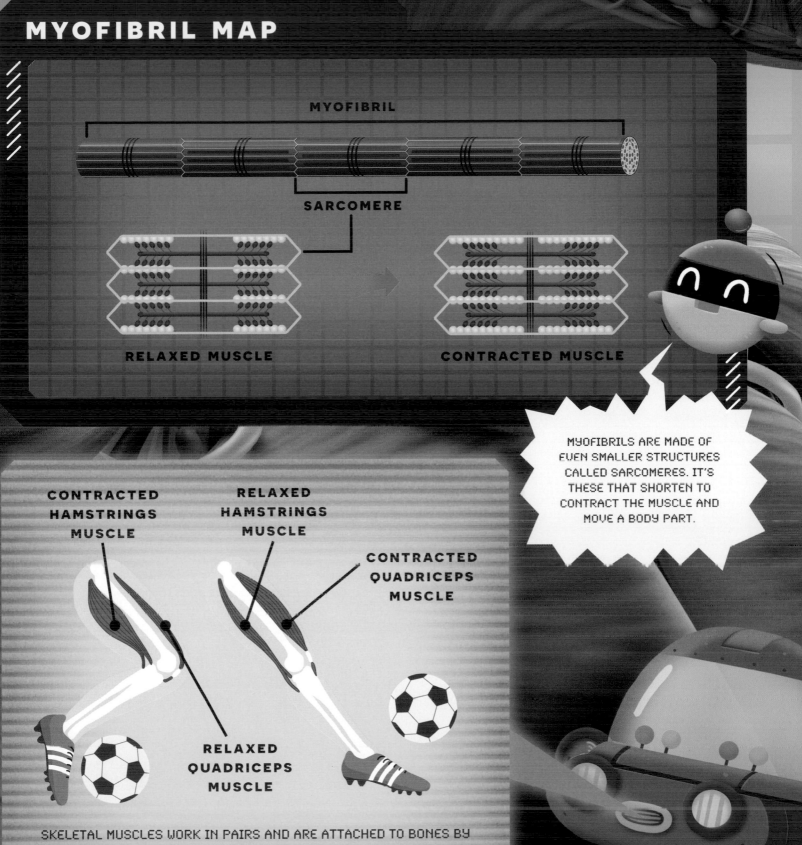

MYOFIBRIL

SARCOMERE

RELAXED MUSCLE

CONTRACTED MUSCLE

CONTRACTED HAMSTRINGS MUSCLE

RELAXED HAMSTRINGS MUSCLE

CONTRACTED QUADRICEPS MUSCLE

RELAXED QUADRICEPS MUSCLE

MYOFIBRILS ARE MADE OF EVEN SMALLER STRUCTURES CALLED SARCOMERES. IT'S THESE THAT SHORTEN TO CONTRACT THE MUSCLE AND MOVE A BODY PART.

SKELETAL MUSCLES WORK IN PAIRS AND ARE ATTACHED TO BONES BY **TENDONS**. WHEN ONE MUSCLE IN THE PAIR CONTRACTS, IT PULLS ON THE BONE, MOVING IT. THEN, WHEN THE OTHER MUSCLE CONTRACTS, IT PULLS THE BONE IN THE OPPOSITE DIRECTION, MOVING IT THE OTHER WAY.

MUSCLE PAIRS

Welcome to the muscle show in the upper arm! Take your seats and get ready for the lifting event. Performing today for you are a muscle pair—the biceps and the triceps.

BICEPS

Hallux is down on the triceps to explain more, while I'm up here on the biceps.

TRICEPS

The brain has sent an instruction to the muscles to raise the forearm in order to lift an apple to the mouth. The muscle fibers in the biceps contract and pull on the forearm, raising it.

Over here on the triceps side, things are calm. There's no effort required from the muscle fibers right now, so they are happy to stay long and relaxed.

A bite is taken from the apple and the body is ready to move it away from the mouth.

The brain sends a message to tell the triceps to contract, in order to lower the arm.

The triceps pulls, the biceps relaxes, and the arm is lowered.

It'll happen all over again when the body is ready to take another bite!

THE SKELETON

Now we've seen the body's muscles, the next section of our tour will be the skeleton. The skeleton is the body's frame—it holds it up, helps it to move, and provides protection. It is made up of lots of individual bones. Bones can't move without muscles, and muscles need bones to hold them in position, so the skeletal system and muscular system work closely together.

FACT FLASH_ The body actually has around 300 bones at birth, but some of these fuse together over time to make up the 206 bones in an adult skeleton.

SKULL
IT PROTECTS
THE BRAIN!

The skeleton is made up of 206 bones, and it extends all around the body. Hard bones provide protection for the soft organs that sit beneath them. And where bones meet each other there's a **joint**, which allows the body to bend and move.

RIBS
THE HEART
AND LUNGS ARE
PROTECTED BY
24 RIBS.

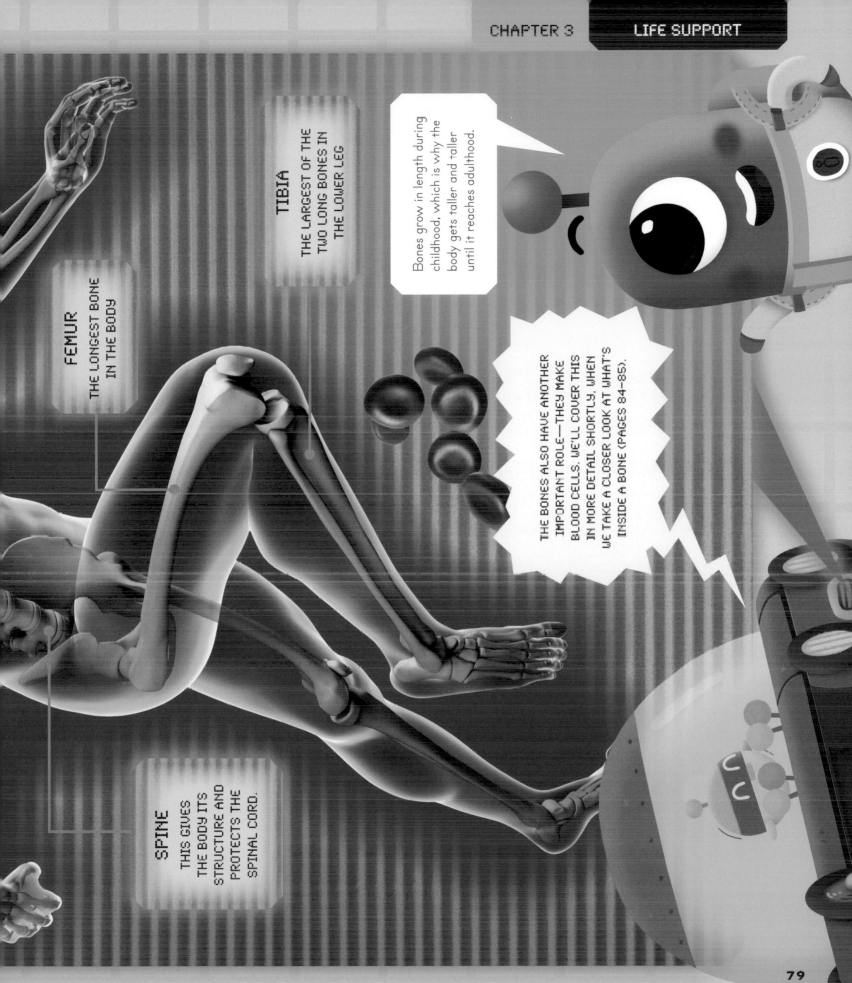

FEMUR
THE LONGEST BONE IN THE BODY

TIBIA
THE LARGEST OF THE TWO LONG BONES IN THE LOWER LEG

SPINE
THIS GIVES THE BODY ITS STRUCTURE AND PROTECTS THE SPINAL CORD.

Bones grow in length during childhood, which is why the body gets taller and taller until it reaches adulthood.

THE BONES ALSO HAVE ANOTHER IMPORTANT ROLE—THEY MAKE BLOOD CELLS. WE'LL COVER THIS IN MORE DETAIL SHORTLY, WHEN WE TAKE A CLOSER LOOK AT WHAT'S INSIDE A BONE (PAGES 84–85).

THE SKULL

The first stop on our tour of the skeleton is the skull. This is one of the most complex parts of the skeleton, as it's made of 22 bones that all sit tightly together to protect the delicate brain and eyes and form the face. The top half is like a helmet covering the brain, and the lower half shapes the facial features and allows the jaw to move.

The dome of the skull wraps up and over the brain and consists of the cranial bones. Babies have spaces between their cranial bones so that their heads can be squished a little as they are born. But adult cranial bones are locked together by joints called sutures.

NASAL CAVITY

UPPER JAW

LOWER JAW

SKULL DEVELOPMENT

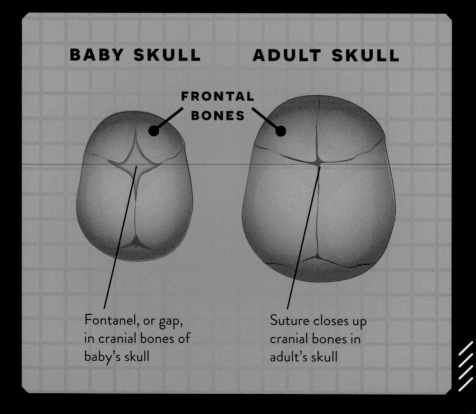

BABY SKULL   ADULT SKULL

FRONTAL BONES

Fontanel, or gap, in cranial bones of baby's skull

Suture closes up cranial bones in adult's skull

FRONTAL BONE

EYE SOCKET

These big chambers within the skull are sockets for the eyeballs to sit in.

AT THE TOP OF THE SKULL WE CAN SEE THE FRONTAL BONE. THIS IS WHAT SHAPES THE FOREHEAD. THE UPPER JAW FORMS THE BASE OF THE EYE SOCKET AND HAS THE TOP TEETH FIXED INTO IT. THE LOWER JAW, ALSO KNOWN AS THE MANDIBLE, IS THE SECTION OF THE SKULL THAT MOVES. THIS ALLOWS THE BODY TO EAT, SPEAK, AND BREATHE, AND IT CONTAINS THE LOWER TEETH.

OPENING FOR NERVES

FACT FLASH_The nasal cavity is a hole in the skull where there are no bones, so air can flow into the body. The nose has a firm shape because it is made of cartilage.

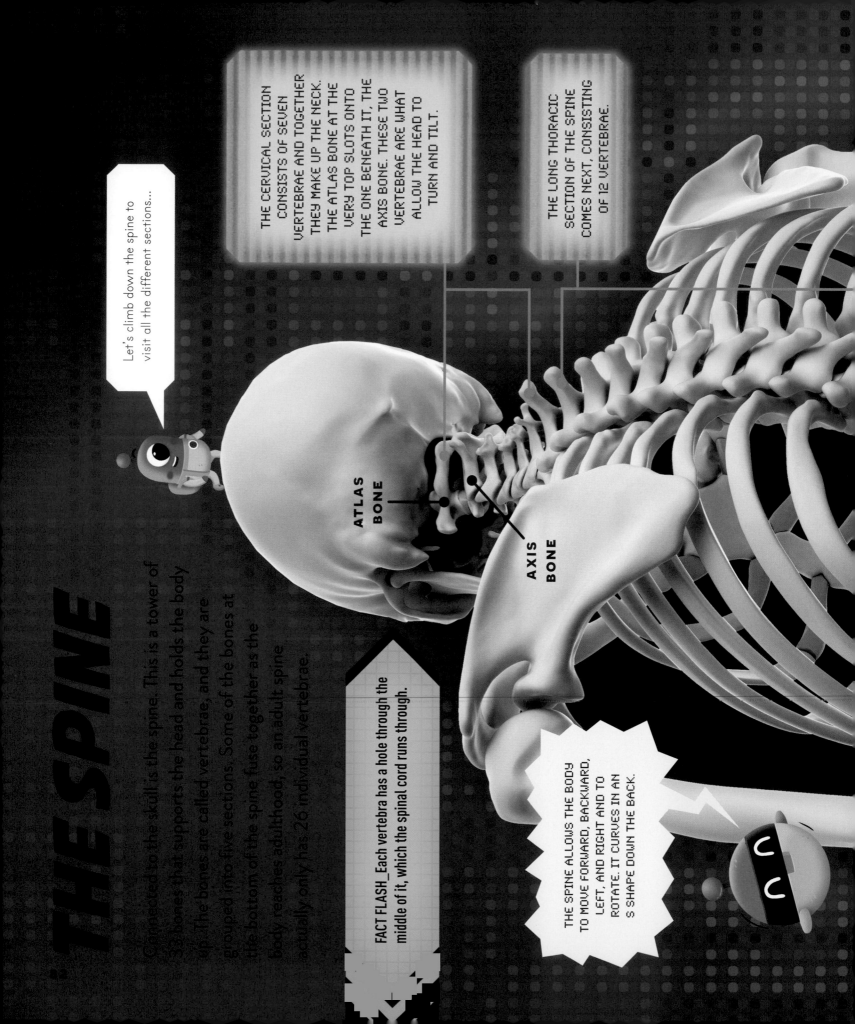

THE SPINE

Connected to the skull is the spine. This is a tower of 33 bones that supports the head and holds the body up. The bones are called vertebrae, and they are grouped into five sections. Some of the bones at the bottom of the spine fuse together as the body reaches adulthood, so an adult spine actually only has 26 individual vertebrae.

Let's climb down the spine to visit all the different sections...

THE CERVICAL SECTION CONSISTS OF SEVEN VERTEBRAE AND TOGETHER THEY MAKE UP THE NECK. THE ATLAS BONE AT THE VERY TOP SLOTS ONTO THE ONE BENEATH IT, THE AXIS BONE. THESE TWO VERTEBRAE ARE WHAT ALLOW THE HEAD TO TURN AND TILT.

THE LONG THORACIC SECTION OF THE SPINE COMES NEXT, CONSISTING OF 12 VERTEBRAE.

ATLAS BONE

AXIS BONE

FACT FLASH_Each vertebra has a hole through the middle of it, which the spinal cord runs through.

THE SPINE ALLOWS THE BODY TO MOVE FORWARD, BACKWARD, LEFT, AND RIGHT AND TO ROTATE. IT CURVES IN AN S SHAPE DOWN THE BACK.

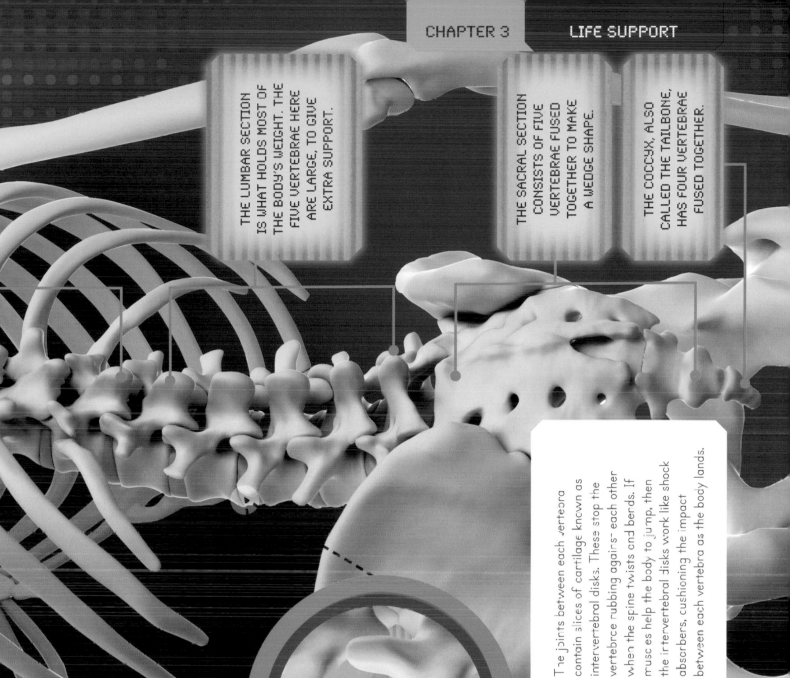

THE LUMBAR SECTION IS WHAT HOLDS MOST OF THE BODY'S WEIGHT. THE FIVE VERTEBRAE HERE ARE LARGE, TO GIVE EXTRA SUPPORT.

THE SACRAL SECTION CONSISTS OF FIVE VERTEBRAE FUSED TOGETHER TO MAKE A WEDGE SHAPE.

THE COCCYX, ALSO CALLED THE TAILBONE, HAS FOUR VERTEBRAE FUSED TOGETHER.

The joints between each vertebra contain slices of cartilage known as intervertebral disks. These stop the vertebrae rubbing against each other when the spine twists and bends. If muscles help the body to jump, then the intervertebral disks work like shock absorbers, cushioning the impact between each vertebra as the body lands.

BONES

The Bodyscope Bus is projecting an image to show how the femur—the largest bone in the body—fits inside the leg. Although bones are hard and strong to give structure to the body, they are not solid. Inside the hard outer shell is a spongy layer, and in that is a jelly-like substance called bone marrow, where blood cells are made.

The outer layer of bone is made of long tubes of hard tissue that run the length of the bone. This is what gives the bone its strength. Arteries and veins run over and under this layer to deliver the nutrients that keep everything working.

FACT FLASH_ Bones need a mineral called calcium to keep them healthy. This comes from foods like dairy, nuts, and... broccoli!

ALTHOUGH THE IMAGE I'M PROJECTING IS ORANGE, THE REAL COLOR OF BONES IS BROWN OR BEIGE—AND NOT WHITE AS MANY PEOPLE THINK.

BONE MARROW IS THE SOFT JELLY-LIKE TISSUE THAT FILLS THE GAPS IN THE SPONGY LAYER. BLOOD CELLS FOR THE ENTIRE BODY ARE MADE HERE. RED MARROW CELLS MAKE RED BLOOD CELLS, WHITE BLOOD CELLS, AND PLATELETS. YELLOW MARROW STORES FAT, WHICH CAN BE BROKEN DOWN AND USED FOR ENERGY IF THE BODY NEEDS IT.

As we can see in the scan below, the spongy layer of bone looks like honeycomb! It works like a shock absorber for some of the body's movements. There are lots of holes within this spongy layer—which is a good thing, because if bones were solid, they would be too heavy to move!

BONE MAP

SPONGY LAYER OF BONE CONTAINING RED BONE MARROW

YELLOW BONE MARROW

BLOOD VESSELS

TYPES OF BONE

Different types of bones have different shapes to help them carry out their jobs. There are five types of bones in total, and the Bodyscope Bus will now give us a presentation on them all.

FLAT BONES

FLAT BONES IN THE SKULL, RIB CAGE, AND PELVIS WORK LIKE A SHIELD TO PROTECT WHATEVER BODY PART IS BEHIND THEM.

STERNUM

IRREGULAR BONES

IRREGULAR BONES ARE JUST THAT—THEY DON'T FIT INTO ANY OTHER CATEGORY. THEY ARE THE VERTEBRAE IN THE SPINE AND THE BONES IN THE PELVIS. THEY HAVE COMPLEX SHAPES AS THEY ARE SPECIALLY DESIGNED TO FIT AROUND AND PROTECT IMPORTANT ORGANS.

VERTEBRA

SHORT BONES

SHORT BONES ARE SHAPED A BIT LIKE A CUBE. THEY ARE FOUND IN THE WRIST AND ANKLE JOINTS AND PROVIDE STABILITY AND A SMALL AMOUNT OF MOVEMENT.

CUNEIFORM

LONG BONES

LONG BONES IN THE ARMS, FINGERS, LEGS, AND TOES ARE THERE TO SUPPORT THE WEIGHT OF THE BODY AND HELP IT MOVE.

FEMUR

SESAMOID BONES

THESE BONES ARE EMBEDDED IN THE TENDONS THAT HOLD LONG BONES AND MUSCLES TOGETHER. THEY CAN BE FOUND IN PLACES LIKE THE HANDS, KNEES, AND FEET AND PROTECT THE TENDONS FROM WEAR AND TEAR. THE KNEECAP, ALSO KNOWN AS THE PATELLA, IS ONE EXAMPLE.

PATELLA

FRACTURE REPAIR

1
BLOOD CLOT

2
NEW BLOOD VESSELS
SOFT CALLUS

3
HARDENING CALLUS

4
HEALED FRACTURE

The outer layer of bone is hard, so it can get chipped, split, or even snap completely. What happens then, Hallux?

Good question, Dewlap. To help understand, look at the diagrams on the screen above. First, the body forms a blood clot around the broken bone, which delivers the cells the bone needs to repair itself. New blood vessels are created, and tissue forms over the break, creating a protective layer called a callus. The callus is soft to begin with, then hardens while new bone begins to grow in its place.

JOINTS

FEMUR

PATELLA

Where bones meet they are connected by joints, such as this one in the knee. This joint allows the bones above and below it to move. There are over 400 joints in the human body and most of them move in one way or another.

The femur is above us, and the shin bone, or tibia, is below us. Hold on tight—the body is about to sit down!

TIBIA

HINGE JOINT

There, the femur has moved and is now in a horizontal position.

Clever design means each joint is specific to the type of movement the bones around it need to do. The knee is a hinge joint, meaning it can only open and close in one direction —a bit like a door.

If we look closely, we can see that the bones don't actually touch each other at a joint. They are held near to each other by **ligaments**, which are like elastic straps.

LIGAMENT

On the end of each bone is the smooth, rubbery substance called cartilage, plus there's some fluid in the area created by the joint, which works like a cushion. This means the bones can move smoothly around each other. However, if the cartilage wears away, the bones will rub together and cause pain for the body.

CARTILAGE

Now we've seen how the knee joint works, here's some information about other types of joints found in the body!

BALL-AND-SOCKET
The round end of one bone fits into the cup end of another. This is like the hip and shoulder joints, where movement in all directions is possible.

SADDLE
This joint allows movement back and forth and side to side, but not rotation. An example is the base of the thumb.

CONDYLOID
This joint allows movement in many directions, but not rotation, like in the jaw and fingers.

PIVOT
This is where one bone swivels around the ring formed by another bone. It happens with the atlas and axis bones (see page 82) at the very top of the spinal column.

GLIDING
The clue is in the name. In gliding joints, such as in the wrist, flat or slightly curved bones slide over each other.

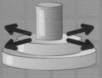

CALF MUSCLE

Hello, I'm reporting from the Achilles tendon. It connects the calf muscle to the heel bone and is the largest tendon in the body! Tendons are like rope, linking the muscle to the bone. Tendons don't stretch as much as muscles, so it's quite common for them to become strained if overworked.

Ligaments form around joints and hold two bones in position next to each other, so they move in the right way. Sometimes they also wrap around tendons, keeping them stable, like this one.

LIGAMENT

ACHILLES TENDON

ANKLE BONE

LIGAMENT

HEEL BONE

UNSUNG HEROES

We've heard all about bones and muscles, but now it's time to talk about the unsung heroes that help them do what they do—the tendons, ligaments, and cartilage. To recap the headlines for you: tendons connect muscle to bone, whereas ligaments attach bone to bone. Cartilage is strong, flexible, gel-like tissue found between bones throughout the body.

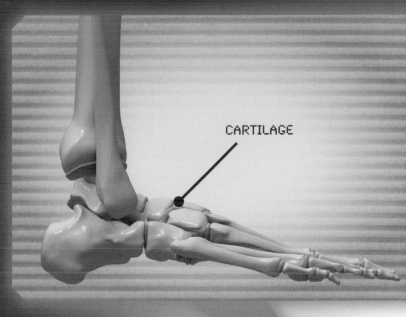

CARTILAGE

TENDON

CARTILAGE DOESN'T HAVE BLOOD VESSELS OR NERVES RUNNING THROUGH IT, BUT IT SITS IN A TYPE OF GEL THAT GIVES IT NUTRIENTS AND MEANS IT IS SOFT. CARTILAGE IS FOUND AT THE END OF BONES TO STOP THEM RUBBING AGAINST EACH OTHER. IT'S ALSO IN THE EAR AND NOSE TO GIVE THEM STRUCTURE WHERE THERE ISN'T BONE.

SPARE PARTS

If the Bodyscope Bus breaks down, we can identify the faulty part, quickly replace it, and get it running like new again. But what about the body? Are there spare parts to keep it running smoothly? We know the heart, lungs, muscles, and bones work hard every single day—what happens if they wear out?

Luckily the body can repair much of itself by producing new cells to fix tissue, bones, and muscles. But some body parts are too big to fully regenerate—if a finger is chopped off or an adult tooth falls out, the body can't just grow a new one. The same can be said about some organs. If one fails, a transplant may be needed.

The Bodyscope Bus is once again using its projector, this time to show how a ball-and-socket joint (page 89) fits into the hip at the top of the leg. Constant use through walking, running, and jumping means that it may eventually become worn, damaged, and painful. That's when a hip replacement might be needed.

THE HIP IN THIS DIAGRAM HAS BEEN REPLACED BY A SHINY NEW METAL ONE THAT WILL LAST FOR MANY MORE YEARS. HIP TRANSPLANTS ARE RELATIVELY COMMON IN OLDER BODIES. MODERN TECHNOLOGY MEANS SURGEONS CAN REMOVE DAMAGED SECTIONS OF THE HIP AND REPLACE THEM WITH METAL, CERAMIC, OR HARD PLASTIC PARTS.

THERE ARE MANY OTHER REPLACEMENT BODY PARTS AVAILABLE, CALLED PROSTHESES. THESE ARE MADE FROM A RANGE OF MATERIALS. PROSTHETIC LEGS AND ARMS CAN BE CREATED USING STRONG, LIGHTWEIGHT MATERIALS LIKE CARBON FIBER AND ALUMINUM. RUBBERY MATERIALS LIKE SILICONE ARE USED FOR PROSTHETIC EARS AND NOSES, WHILE REPLACEMENT TEETH ARE USUALLY MADE OF HARD ACRYLIC OR PORCELAIN.

STAYING SAFE

Our tour is progressing quickly! We're now pleased to welcome you to the section that will show off the body's defense mechanisms and communications devices. But we'll need to be careful during our visit of the immune system. The body is always ready to defend itself against obvious attackers like germs, but foreign bodies like us may also set off the alarm bells!

SIGHTS TO SPOT.................

ANTIBODIES: PROTEINS THAT STICK TO HARMFUL GERMS AND TELL WHITE BLOOD CELLS TO ATTACK THEM

LYMPH NODES: SMALL ORGANS THAT ARE PART OF THE IMMUNE SYSTEM AND HELP PRODUCE THE WHITE BLOOD CELLS THAT FIGHT GERMS

SCABS: SHIELDS THAT FORM ON THE OUTSIDE OF THE SKIN TO PROTECT IT FROM GERMS WHILE IT IS HEALING

BODY MAPS

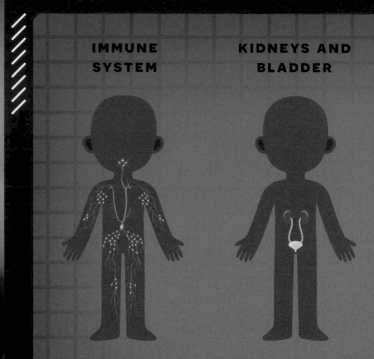

IMMUNE SYSTEM

A network of cells, tissues, and organs that defends the body against attack.

KIDNEYS AND BLADDER

These are organs that help remove waste products from the body.

We'll be traveling around many different areas of the body in this part of the tour.

WHITE BLOOD CELL

SKIN, HAIR, AND NAILS

Together, these interconnected elements make up the body's outer covering.

THROAT AND VOICE BOX

These are the areas that help the body speak, shout, and sing.

THE SKIN IS THE BODY'S FIRST LINE OF DEFENSE, ACTING LIKE A PROTECTIVE LAYER OVER WHAT'S INSIDE. KEEPING IT CLEAN IS IMPORTANT, AS GERMS CAN EASILY BE TRANSFERRED INTO THE BODY FROM THE SKIN THROUGH ACCESS POINTS, SUCH AS THE EYES OR MOUTH.

Careful with the white blood cells! They're an important part of the immune system!

IMMUNE SYSTEM

Let us introduce you to the immune system, the body's internal defense mechanism. It's made up of various parts, including white blood cells, the lymphatic system, and a number of organs. The main soldiers in this army are the white blood cells, which can hunt down and destroy germs. They're also very intelligent —they remember how to protect the body against germs they've battled before.

LYMPHOCYTE

FACT FLASH_A single drop of blood can contain 25,000 white blood cells!

There are many different types of white blood cells, all of which do different jobs. Two of the main types are lymphocytes and phagocytes. This is a lymphocyte.

Lymphocytes look for proteins on the surface of germs that the body doesn't recognize. If it finds such a protein, called an **antigen**, it then produces an **antibody** that sticks to the germs and signals to the phagocytes to come and engulf them.

ATTACKING BACTERIA

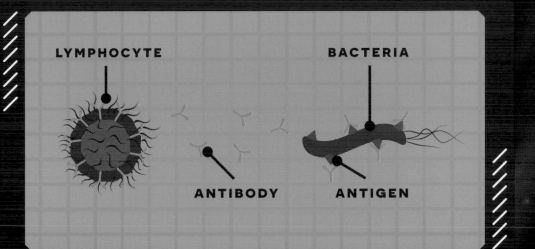

LYMPHOCYTE   BACTERIA

ANTIBODY   ANTIGEN

Phagocytes are attracted to germs and destroy them by surrounding them, swallowing them up, and breaking them down. We'll be seeing them in action soon (page 100).

WHITE BLOOD CELLS ARE ABLE TO FIND GERMS BY FOLLOWING THE CHEMICAL TRAILS THEY LEAVE BEHIND. THE CELLS TRAVEL AROUND IN THE BLOODSTREAM AND THE LYMPH, WHICH IS A CLEAR LIQUID THAT PASSES THROUGH TISSUES IN THE BODY (PAGES 102–103).

SOMETIMES THE BODY THINKS AN INVADER IS ATTACKING IT, BUT REALLY IT'S JUST A HARMLESS SUBSTANCE—LIKE FOOD, POLLEN, DUST... OR US! IF THE BODY MISTAKENLY REACTS TO A SUBSTANCE LIKE THIS, IT'S CALLED AN **ALLERGY**.

INVADERS

The word "germ" is the general term for all minuscule **microorganisms** that try to invade the body. Some can cause mild diseases that lead to sneezing and coughing, while others can cause serious illnesses. Germs are teeny-tiny, which allows them to enter cells and then **reproduce** inside them. There are various types of germs—let's see how many we can find.

INSIDE THE RED BLOOD CELL BELOW ARE A COUPLE OF INVADERS CALLED PROTISTS. THESE ARE SINGLE-CELL PARASITES, WHICH MEANS THEY FEED ON OTHER LIVING THINGS. THESE PROTISTS CAUSE THE DISEASE MALARIA. THEY BEGIN LIFE INSIDE A MOSQUITO. IF THE INSECT BITES A HUMAN, THE PROTISTS ENTER THE BODY, TAKING OVER RED BLOOD CELLS TO CAUSE ILLNESS.

CORONAVIRUS

PROTIST

Let's begin with a virus. Viruses cause common illnesses such as colds and flu, and also more serious diseases like measles. This is a coronavirus, which causes an illness called COVID-19. The virus travels in a little droplet that can easily enter the body through the nose or mouth. This is how the body can catch a virus from another person if they cough or sneeze. When the virus enters cells in the body, it multiplies, making the body unwell.

SALMONELLA

FUNGI

We might have passed some helpful bacteria when we were visiting the digestive system, but nasty bacteria can also enter the body in food and drink, causing vomiting and diarrhea. Bacteria such as salmonella can produce poisonous **toxins**.

When you think of fungi, you probably think of mushrooms that like to grow in soil. But some types of fungi can also grow on the body. Usually, they take up home on the skin in places that tend to get damp and warm, like in between the toes. Athlete's foot is caused by one such fungus. It's an infection that causes the skin on the toes to become flaky and itchy.

ATTACK!

PHAGOCYTE

GERM

OK everyone, we've stopped here in the bloodstream to witness a white blood cell in action! This is a phagocyte —the type of white blood cell that kills germs by swallowing them.

Look, it's spotted a germ. It's probably best to stand back and make sure we don't get swallowed up as well!

This particular phagocyte is called a neutrophil. Around 70 percent of white blood cells are neutrophils, so they're pretty common.

When infection strikes, neutrophils are always first on the scene. Watch closely—as the neutrophil approaches the germ, it opens itself up.

Gulp! It's now engulfed the germ, dragging it inside the cell.

Stand back, Dewlap! There'd be no escaping if you got swallowed as well!

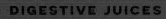

LYMPHATIC SYSTEM

The lymphatic system is part of the immune system —a system within a system—and it works alongside the circulatory system! It is essentially a network of drainage vessels. Its role is to drain a fluid called **lymph** from the tissues, check it for any unwanted intruders, and return it to the bloodstream along with new white blood cells called lymphocytes. By doing this, fluid levels in the body are maintained and tissue cells are cleaned of waste.

Here I am, sitting on a lymph node. Lymph nodes are little hubs located all over the body's network of lymph vessels. They work to clean the lymph fluid as it passes through them. They also make lymphocytes and other immune system cells that track down and destroy viruses and bacteria.

FACT FLASH_ Capillary walls are so thin that water and proteins often leak out into the tissues surrounding them. If the tissues weren't drained by the lymphatic system, they would swell up and cause complications such as mobility issues and skin problems.

ARTERY

LYMPH VESSEL

VEIN

Like blood vessels, lymph vessels run all over the body. They work with a number of organs to make up the lymphatic system, including the bone marrow, thymus gland, spleen, tonsils, and appendix. Lymphocytes made by the lymphatic system are fed into the bloodstream by the lymph, so the body is ready to defend itself at any moment.

BODY MAP

LYMPHATIC SYSTEM

THYMUS GLAND

TONSILS

LYMPH NODE

SPLEEN

APPENDIX

BONE MARROW

LYMPH FLUID

LYMPH

DIRECTION OF FLOW

VALVE CLOSED   VALVE OPEN

LYMPH ONLY FLOWS IN ONE DIRECTION —UP TOWARD THE NECK. VALVES PREVENT IT FLOWING IN THE OPPOSITE DIRECTION. ONCE IN THE NECK, IT IS ABLE TO ENTER THE BLOODSTREAM AGAIN THROUGH TWO VEINS.

HELPING HANDS

The body does an amazing job of protecting itself and fighting off invaders using its own immune system. It also knows how to repair itself. But there's no problem with also asking for independent help sometimes! Health professionals look at ways they can help prevent the body from taking a hit in the first place.

We're back in a blood vessel, this time in the arm. That giant needle looks scary but it's actually doing the body good, as it's delivering **medicine** for a **vaccination**.

A vaccine contains chemicals that teach the immune system how to react to a disease before it is actually infected with it. By teaching the cells how to fight a particular virus, they'll know exactly how to respond should the real germ enter the body, so they can destroy the disease more quickly.

SOMETIMES THE BODY NEEDS A HELPING HAND TO BLOCK OUT PAIN AFTER AN INJURY OR INFECTION HAS TAKEN PLACE, IN THE FORM OF A PAINKILLER. WHEN CELLS ARE DAMAGED OR INJURED, THEY RELEASE CHEMICALS CALLED PROSTAGLANDINS. THESE ARE PICKED UP BY NERVE CELLS AND MESSAGES ARE QUICKLY SENT TO THE BRAIN TO TELL IT WHERE THE PAIN IS, HOW MUCH IT HURTS, AND HOW TO REACT. PAINKILLERS STOP CELLS FROM RELEASING THE PROSTAGLANDIN FOR A WHILE, ONCE THE BRAIN HAS GOT THE MESSAGE.

TABLET PAINKILLER

LIQUID PAINKILLER

MANY DIFFERENT TYPES OF MEDICINES CAN HELP THE BODY RECOVER FROM ILLNESS. ANTIBIOTICS CAN FIGHT BACTERIAL INFECTIONS, FOR EXAMPLE. BUT ONE OF THE SIMPLEST WAYS TO KEEP THE BODY STRONG IS TO HAVE A HEALTHY LIFESTYLE. A DIET CONTAINING LOTS OF FRUITS AND VEGETABLES, REGULAR EXERCISE, AND PLENTY OF SLEEP WILL ALL HELP THE BODY TO FUNCTION SMOOTHLY.

THE KIDNEYS

We've arrived at the two kidneys. These organs are the body's waste management system, responsible for cleaning the blood. Just like in the digestive system, there are excess salts, toxins, and water that need to be removed from the bloodstream to keep it working effectively.

Blood flows into the kidneys from the renal artery. It passes into an area called the cortex, where tiny filters called nephrons remove all the waste from the blood. This waste is a fluid called urine. The clean blood then flows out of the kidneys via the renal vein.

KIDNEY MAP

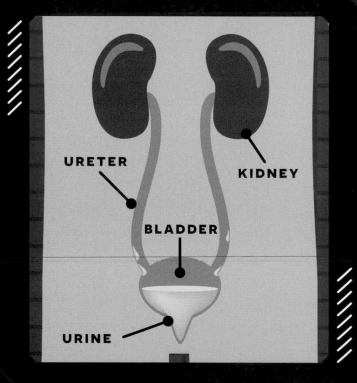

URETER

KIDNEY

BLADDER

URINE

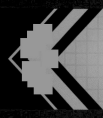

FACT FLASH_Although urine is mostly made of water, it has a yellow color due to chemicals found in old blood cells that need to be filtered out of the bloodstream.

CORTEX

RENAL VEIN

MEDULLA (MADE UP OF RENAL PYRAMIDS)

NEXT, URINE FLOWS INTO THE CENTRAL AREA OF THE KIDNEYS, CALLED THE MEDULLA. THIS IS MADE UP OF SEVERAL SMALLER STRUCTURES CALLED RENAL PYRAMIDS. THEY CHANNEL THE URINE TOWARD THE RENAL PELVIS, WHICH THEN FLOWS INTO A TUBE CALLED THE URETER.

RENAL PELVIS

RENAL ARTERY

Finally, the urine flows down the ureter and into the bladder. The bladder is a muscular bag that holds the urine until the body is ready to release it via the urethra (or, to put it another way, is ready to take a pee).

URETER

SKIN

OK everyone, it's time to travel outside of the body for a short period. We're visiting the skin, hair, and nails next—and it's best if we view these from above! We tend to think of organs as things inside the body, but the skin is actually the body's largest organ. Its job is protection and temperature regulation. The skin is also loaded with nerve cells, giving the body the important sense of touch.

FACT FLASH_Places like the soles of the feet have thicker epidermis layers for extra protection.

We are standing on the outer, waterproof layer of skin, known as the epidermis. It's where hair, nails, and **sweat** glands reach the surface, and its main function is to protect everything beneath it. The cells in the epidermis layer are constantly flaking off, but new ones are being made all the time to replace them.

THE SKIN IS ACTUALLY MADE UP OF THREE LAYERS OF TISSUE: THE EPIDERMIS, THE DERMIS, AND A LAYER OF FATTY TISSUE THAT CONNECTS IT ALL TO THE MUSCLES BELOW.

SKIN MAP

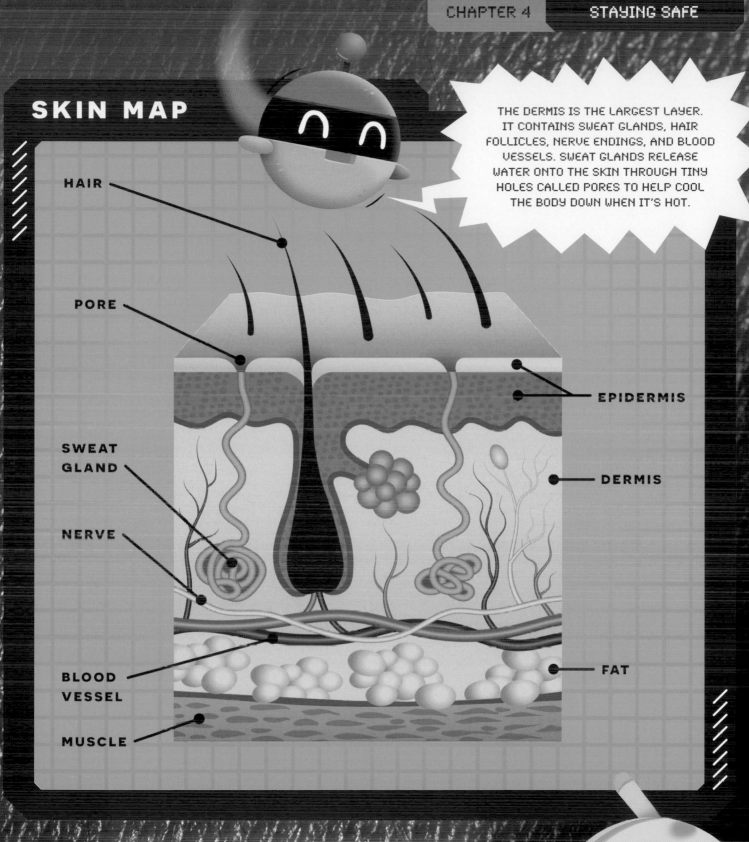

HAIR

PORE

SWEAT GLAND

NERVE

BLOOD VESSEL

MUSCLE

EPIDERMIS

DERMIS

FAT

THE DERMIS IS THE LARGEST LAYER. IT CONTAINS SWEAT GLANDS, HAIR FOLLICLES, NERVE ENDINGS, AND BLOOD VESSELS. SWEAT GLANDS RELEASE WATER ONTO THE SKIN THROUGH TINY HOLES CALLED PORES TO HELP COOL THE BODY DOWN WHEN IT'S HOT.

The fat layer is there to help with temperature regulation, and for padding. Its thickness depends on the area of the body. Fat also stores energy, which the body can break down and use when it needs it.

BUMPS AND CUTS

The skin is the body's first line of defense, so it's prone to damage. Bumps, cuts, burns, grazes—these are all common problems, but luckily the skin is a clever organ! It can fix most minor injuries all by itself, and it fully regenerates each month, which means it completely replaces itself by growing new skin cells.

When the body bumps into something and gets a knock, some of the small blood vessels in the skin break, causing a bruise. The dark color of a bruise on the skin is red blood cells that have leaked out from the damaged blood vessel and collected under the epidermis layer. The color of a bruise changes as the body breaks down these blood cells and disposes of them via the kidneys' cleaning process.

SKIN REPAIR

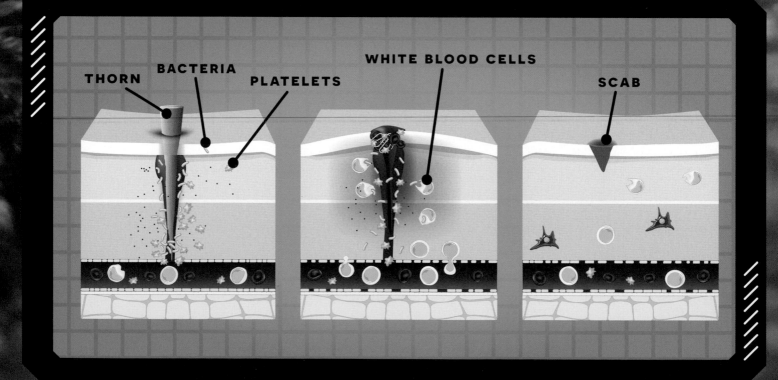

THORN   BACTERIA   PLATELETS   WHITE BLOOD CELLS   SCAB

If the skin gets cut, the body sounds the alarm! This is a major breach in its defenses and germs can easily enter, so things happen fast. Platelets in the blood rush to the wound and seal up the gap as quickly as possible. This creates a scab on the surface of the skin. White blood cells also arrive to attack any bacteria. As the skin regenerates itself over the following days and weeks, the new skin tissue shows as a **scar**.

IF A WOUND IS VERY DEEP OR WIDE, THE BODY MIGHT NEED A BIT OF HELP. STITCHES PUT IN BY A NURSE OR DOCTOR HOLD THE EDGES OF THE CUT SKIN TOGETHER TO ALLOW THE HEALING PROCESS TO BEGIN.

WOUND HEALING USING STITCHES

STITCHES, ALSO KNOWN AS SUTURES, ARE THREADED THROUGH THE SKIN EITHER SIDE OF THE WOUND.

ONCE THE WOUND HAS STARTED TO HEAL, THE STITCHES ARE REMOVED OR NATURALLY DISSOLVE.

THE WOUND CONTINUES TO HEAL AND NEW SKIN TISSUE CREATES A SCAR, WHICH WILL FADE OVER TIME.

111

HAIR AND NAILS

Hair and nails grow out of the dermis layer of skin (page 109). Both help the skin in protecting the body, and both are made of a strong protein called keratin. Hair covers almost the entire body, but in some areas it grows much longer and the individual hairs are closer together. Nails can be found at the tips of the fingers, thumbs, and toes.

We are in a forest of hairs, so we must be on top of the head. Hair follicles here are close together, which means the head has lots of hair to help protect the delicate scalp. Hair color is decided before birth. Later in life, it turns gray as the cells that produce the color in the hair age and die.

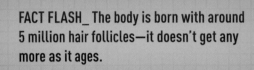

FACT FLASH_ The body is born with around 5 million hair follicles—it doesn't get any more as it ages.

Each hair is controlled by an organ in the skin called a follicle. The shape of the follicle determines if the hair is straight, wavy, or curly. The hair follicle contains living cells that grow hair at a rate of around 0.5 in. (1 cm) each month. But by the time the hair reaches the outside of the body, the cells forming the strand have died—which is why nothing can be felt through it. Next to each follicle is a sebaceous gland, which secretes a lubricating oil called sebum onto the hair.

HAIR TYPES

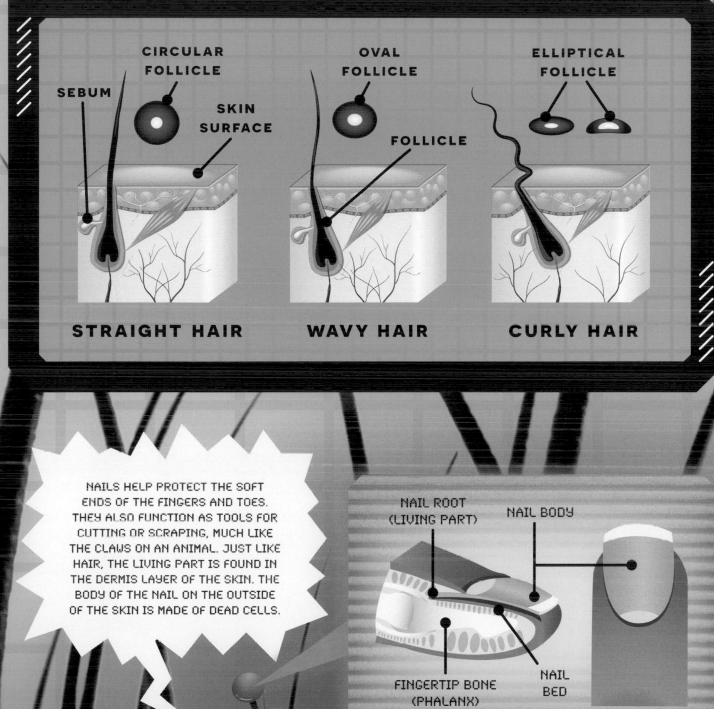

SEBUM — CIRCULAR FOLLICLE — SKIN SURFACE — **STRAIGHT HAIR**

OVAL FOLLICLE — FOLLICLE — **WAVY HAIR**

ELLIPTICAL FOLLICLE — **CURLY HAIR**

NAILS HELP PROTECT THE SOFT ENDS OF THE FINGERS AND TOES. THEY ALSO FUNCTION AS TOOLS FOR CUTTING OR SCRAPING, MUCH LIKE THE CLAWS ON AN ANIMAL. JUST LIKE HAIR, THE LIVING PART IS FOUND IN THE DERMIS LAYER OF THE SKIN. THE BODY OF THE NAIL ON THE OUTSIDE OF THE SKIN IS MADE OF DEAD CELLS.

NAIL ROOT (LIVING PART) — NAIL BODY — FINGERTIP BONE (PHALANX) — NAIL BED

Hello! We've taken a short stroll from the top of the head to one of the eyes. This is where we'll investigate the interesting fluid that leaks out of them... tears!

Tears are the body's liquid soldiers, protecting the eyes from infection.

LACRIMAL GLAND

Using the Bodyscope Bus's scanner, I've pinpointed the area where tears are made. Here, under the outer edge of the eyelid, sits the lacrimal gland.

This gland makes between 15 and 28 gallons (70 and 130 liters) of tears every year! The eyes are constantly producing a type of tear known as basal tears. These form a film over the eye to keep it lubricated and protect it from debris, like dust and dirt.

Here come some tears... I'd better put my umbrella up! Reflex tears form when the eye is exposed to irritants, like smoke.

I've collected a sample and can see that tears are made up of water, salts, fatty oils, and lots of proteins. However, the most important ingredient is the chemical **enzyme** lysozyme, as this can destroy bacteria! The eye may become irritated if bacteria is not killed by the tears.

MUCOUS LAYER

AQUEOUS LAYER

LIPID LAYER

There's a third type of tear that's produced when the body experiences intense feelings. These are called emotional tears.

Looking through the magnifying glass at the tear film that covers the eye, we can see that it's made up of three layers. The sticky mucous layer keeps the tear attached to the eye. The middle aqueous layer hydrates the eye, keeps bacteria away, and protects the cornea. The outer oily lipid layer prevents the other layers from evaporating.

After the lacrimal glands have produced tears and they've washed over the eye, the tears drain away through tear ducts located at the inner corner of the eye.

If the tear ducts become blocked, the eye can become watery and irritated.

OK, Dewlap, it's time to head back into the body. The tear ducts run into the nasal cavity, where the liquid then gets swallowed down the throat. Let's go follow it... Off we go!

THE THROAT

Here we are, at the back of the mouth, looking down the throat. The tears that flowed down here with us have been swallowed into the stomach, but we're going to stick around for a little bit longer to explore.

All that slimy stuff is mucus. And it looks like Bot got stuck! Mucus is very sticky. It's the body's flypaper, used for trapping germs and dirt. Little cilia hairs lining the throat move it around to make sure there's a good coating. While we try and rescue Bot, let's learn more about this mucus.

THE THROAT, ALSO KNOWN AS THE PHARYNX, STARTS BEHIND THE NOSE, GOES DOWN THE NECK, AND ENDS AT THE TOP OF THE TRACHEA (THE WINDPIPE). IT IS A MUSCULAR TUBE USED AS A PASSAGEWAY FOR AIR, FOOD, LIQUID—AND MUCUS!

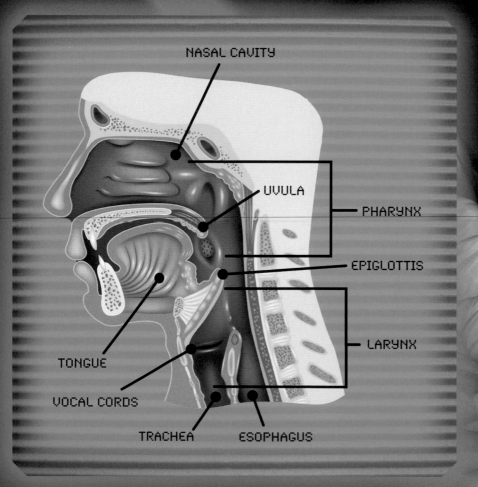

NASAL CAVITY

UVULA

PHARYNX

EPIGLOTTIS

LARYNX

TONGUE

VOCAL CORDS

TRACHEA

ESOPHAGUS

HELP! THE BODY MAKES MORE MUCUS WHEN IT SENSES A THREAT OR CHANGE. THIS CAN BE DUE TO AN INFECTION SUCH AS A COLD OR FLU VIRUSES, ALLERGIES, OR EVEN SPICY FOOD! IF MUCUS TURNS GREEN, THIS IS A SIGN THAT IT'S FIGHTING A WAR AGAINST GERMS, AND THE BODY MAY HAVE A COLD.

FACT FLASH_Mucus is made up of water and proteins, and constantly drips down the back of the throat. Humans swallow about 2.5 pints (1.5 liters) of mucus a day!

Another purpose of mucus is to keep the airways moist so they can function properly. Glands that line the nose and throat produce mucus all day long. Mucus also works with the immune system, as it traps many of the particles the body breathes in. Antibodies and enzymes within the mucus are then ready to fight off the germs.

117

COMMUNICATION

Now we've unstuck Bot from the mucus, we've traveled down the throat to the communication center of the body, the larynx. This is where the body makes its sounds—along with a little help from the diaphragm, the vocal cords, the mouth, and some air, of course. The body uses vocal communication to interact with other people and its surroundings.

WITHIN THE LARYNX ARE TWO FLAPS OF SKIN CALLED VOCAL CORDS, WHICH THE BODY USES TO FORM SOUNDS.

The larynx can be found at the bottom of the throat and the top of the trachea. It is made of cartilage and is also known as the voice box.

This is what the vocal cords in the larynx look like from above. As air is pushed out of the lungs, it passes through the vocal cords. When the body is silent, the two cords are held open by the muscles around them and air passes by smoothly. But when the body wants to speak, the cords contract and restrict the flow of air. The air makes them vibrate, creating sound waves that come out of the mouth as speech.

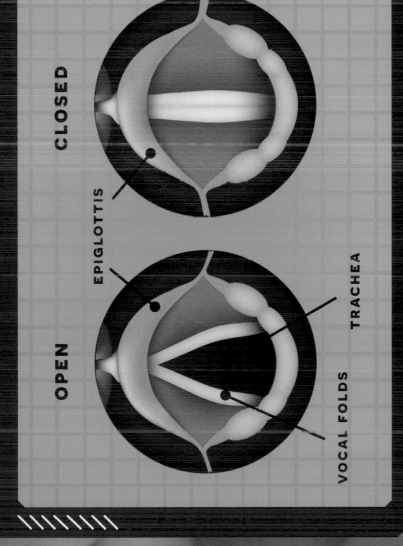

VOCAL CORD MAP

OPEN

CLOSED

EPIGLOTTIS

VOCAL FOLDS

TRACHEA

FACT FLASH_ Sometimes germs cause an infection in the larynx called laryngitis. The vocal cords become inflamed, swollen, or sore, and the voice becomes hoarse—or is even lost completely! Laryngitis can also be caused by overuse or irritation of the vocal cords.

SPEECH

Oooh, the body is speaking! Let's watch, listen, and learn to see how sound is made into speech. The larynx, or voice box, is the source of the sound. But it is the shape of the tongue, teeth, and lips against the vibrating air as it exits the body that turns the sound into units of speech, called phonemes.

Some sounds, like "ss," are created by the tongue pushing up against the roof of the mouth. Others, like "ff," are made by the teeth and lips. The sound from the letters "p" and "t" come from suddenly opening and closing the air pathway.

SPEECH SOUNDS

AH   OOOH   EEE   NUH

BUH   CHUH   OH   FUH

LUH   RAH   THUH

SOUND TRAVELS IN WAVES, LIKE RIPPLES ON WATER. IF THEIR FLOW IS ALTERED BY AN OBSTRUCTION OR A BEND IN THEIR PATH, THEN THEY WILL CHANGE SHAPE TOO. AS SOUND WAVES LEAVE THE LARYNX AND TRAVEL UP THROUGH THE THROAT AND OUT OF THE MOUTH, THEIR SHAPE—AND THE SOUND THEY PRODUCE—IS AFFECTED BY EVERYTHING THEY PASS, INCLUDING THE TONGUE, THE TEETH, AND THE LIPS.

FACT FLASH_In the English language, speech is made up of about 44 phoneme sounds, which are put together to make words. Other languages have different numbers of phoneme sounds.

The vocal cords control how high or low the sound is (this is called pitch) and how loud or quiet it is (volume). The tighter the cords, the less air can pass through them, so the sound becomes higher pitched. And the greater the pressure of air that is blown past the vocal cords, the louder the voice becomes.

NOSE

TONGUE

LIP

TEETH

VOCAL CORDS

SPEECH PATH

SLEEP

We've come back to the brain so we can tell you all about one of the best forms of protection for the body... sleep! Sleep is needed for many reasons, but mostly to let the body and brain repair, restore, and reenergize. Without it, the body's immunity would be weakened, and the brain wouldn't be able to function as well.

There are two main types of sleep—REM and non-REM sleep. The body cycles through periods of both throughout the night, and each cycle of sleep lasts from 90–120 minutes. Non-REM sleep comes first. Muscles relax, brain activity reduces, the heart rate slows, and the body is able to restore itself.

REM sleep happens when brain activity increases again and the eyes start to move a lot (REM stands for "rapid eye movement"). The heart rate speeds up, and the brain processes all its information from the day. This type of sleep is when dreams occur—the eyes dart around, focusing on the dream images.

THE SLEEP CYCLE

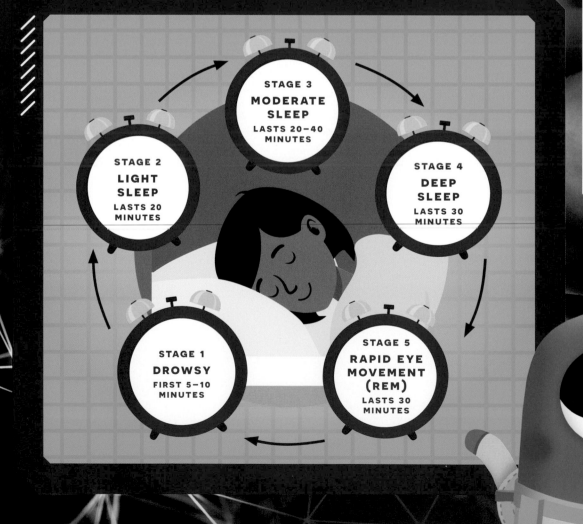

STAGE 3
MODERATE SLEEP
LASTS 20–40 MINUTES

STAGE 2
LIGHT SLEEP
LASTS 20 MINUTES

STAGE 4
DEEP SLEEP
LASTS 30 MINUTES

STAGE 1
DROWSY
FIRST 5–10 MINUTES

STAGE 5
RAPID EYE MOVEMENT (REM)
LASTS 30 MINUTES

PINEAL GLAND

AN INTERNAL "BODY CLOCK" REGULATES THE BODY'S SLEEP CYCLE, SO THE BODY IS NATURALLY READY TO SLEEP AT NIGHT. IT IS CONTROLLED BY HORMONES RELEASED FROM A TINY PART OF THE BRAIN KNOWN AS THE PINEAL GLAND. A HORMONE CALLED MELATONIN MAKES THE BODY DROWSY, AND A HORMONE CALLED CORTISOL PROMOTES ENERGY AND ALERTNESS.

ZZZZZZ

FACT FLASH_ One-third of the body's entire life is spent asleep. Most adults require between seven and nine hours of sleep a night, but children need much more.

KEEPING ON

So, we've made it to the final stage of the tour! Get your magnifying glass at the ready, as it's time to study some truly minuscule cells. Cells are what make everything we've seen before possible. They are both the body's building blocks and its instruction manual. A new body begins when just two single cells unite.

Cells are so tiny we've had to shrink ourselves down A LOT! Although we're now extremely small, there will still be lots to see. Cells are packed full of structures and are constantly buzzing with activity—like mini-cities. Right now, we're on top of a cell. The tentacle-like things behind me are cilia, which help move fluids within (and outside of) the cell.

SIGHTS TO SPOT...............

NUCLEUS: EVEN SMALLER THAN THE CELL ITSELF, THE **NUCLEUS** CONTAINS ALL THE BODY'S PLANS

STEM CELLS: THEY CAN DEVELOP INTO ANY SPECIALIZED CELL THEY LIKE

RARE EGG CELL: ONLY ONE OF THESE IS RELEASED EACH MONTH

FACT FLASH_ About 10,000 human cells could fit on the head of a pin!

AS WE TAKE YOU AROUND A CELL, YOU'LL SEE ITS ORGANELLES, WHICH MEANS "LITTLE ORGANS." THESE ARE STRUCTURES WITHIN A CELL THAT HAVE SPECIFIC JOBS TO DO, JUST LIKE ORGANS WITHIN THE BODY.

As we delve even further, we'll take a look at **DNA**—molecules that carry information about the body's development, function, and growth. Sections of DNA form units called **genes**, which decide the individual features for the body, such as hair and eye color.

CELL SIGHTS

It's time to explore one of the parts of the body that help to hold it all together—a cell. There are more than 200 types of these structures. They group together in families to build tissues, which then build organs, which then combine to create systems, which all work together to make the body function!

We've shrunk down to teeny-tiny cell size, so we can study its inner workings. A cell is the smallest living thing in the entire body and is made up of lots of even smaller structures called organelles. The Bodyscope Bus has highlighted some of the key ones for us...

CENTROSOME
A CYLINDRICAL STRUCTURE THAT HELPS WITH CELL DIVISION

LYSOSOME
A SMALL SPHERICAL STRUCTURE THAT HELPS BREAK DOWN OLD, WORN-OUT CELL PARTS

NUCLEUS
THIS IS THE CONTROL CENTER THAT HOLDS THE INFORMATION ABOUT WHAT TYPE OF CELL IT IS. IT ALSO MAKES RIBOSOMES.

CYTOPLASM
A JELLY-LIKE LIQUID IN WHICH ALL THE PARTS OF THE CELL SIT

GOLGI APPARATUS
THIS IS WHERE PROTEINS ARE PROCESSED READY FOR USE IN THE CELL.

MITOCHONDRIA

THESE ARE THE CELL'S BATTERIES, PROVIDING ENERGY CONVERTED FROM FOOD PASSED TO THEM FROM THE DIGESTIVE SYSTEM.

FACT FLASH_ There are around 100 trillion cells in the body, and 5 million new cells are made every second to replace old ones.

CELL MEMBRANE

THIS SURROUNDS THE CELL AND DECIDES WHAT CAN PASS INTO AND OUT OF THE CELL.

ENDOPLASMIC RETICULUM

A NETWORK OF SACS AND TUBES WHERE MANY OF THE SUBSTANCES THAT THE CELL NEEDS ARE MADE, SUCH AS LIPIDS (FATS) AND CARBOHYDRATES (SUGARS)

RIBOSOMES

TINY STRUCTURES PRODUCING PROTEINS THAT THE CELL THEN EITHER USES OR SENDS OUT INTO THE BODY TO HELP IT FUNCTION

All cells make new cells by dividing themselves. The cell duplicates all of its contents, then splits to form two identical daughter cells in a process called mitosis.

MITOSIS —

Cells come in all different shapes depending on what job they do. Hallux, I'm going to quiz you on some of the ones we've seen around the body to see if you can remember their names! Our first cell is long and thin so it can connect up with others to create pathways all around the body. Any ideas what it is?

Hmm, let me think...

Let's see... there are lots of messages whizzing about in the form of electrical signals. The axon is like a cable that passes information down the cell. And where the cell meets another there's a synapse, where chemicals are made and released to pass on the message... it must be a nerve cell!

AXON

CELL BODY

SYNAPSE

Correct! (See pages 12–13.)

This one is easy because we've seen them in lots of places on the tour! Red blood cells are disks with a flat center that helps them flow through blood vessels.

Well done!

Hmm, thin shapes, bunched together... Oh, and now contracting and becoming shorter. That must mean they are... muscle cells?

Yes, that's right, these are smooth muscle cells (page 73). These ones are lining the walls of the small intestine.

Can you remember seeing these before, Hallux? Do you know what they do?

Sure, Dewlap, these are found in the eye (page 17). They're photoreceptor cells, also known as rods and cones, which detect and absorb light.

This one is round and simple... Hmm, I'm not sure we've seen this before. What does it do, Dewlap?

Sorry, Hallux, this is a trick question. It's a stem cell— a special type of cell that can turn into any type of cell that is needed by the body!

CHROMOSOMES AND DNA

This tour has shown us that the body is a very complex system. We know that, while all bodies function in the same way—breathing and digesting food, for example—each body is also unique. The reason for this is DNA (deoxyribonucleic acid), which holds the information about how everything works and can be found in a cell's nucleus. If you thought cells were tiny, then you'll be amazed at how minuscule DNA is!

After shrinking down even further, we've now entered the cell's nucleus. Just in front of us is a **chromosome**. In most cells, there are 46 chromosomes, divided into 23 pairs. Chromosomes are like bookshelves, holding all the information for the body, and the DNA within them are the books. The human body receives 23 chromosomes from their mother and 23 from their father.

DNA has two strands that twist together into a shape called a helix, which looks a bit like a spiraling ladder. DNA is a molecule made up of four basic chemical building blocks, which form the steps in the ladder shape. These steps are the instructions for the body.

CHROMOSOME MAP

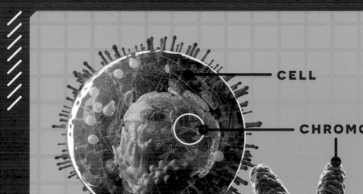

CELL

CHROMOSOME

DNA

GENE

EVERYBODY'S DNA IS UNIQUE, APART FROM THAT OF IDENTICAL TWINS! THEY INHERIT EXACTLY THE SAME DNA WHEN THEY ARE FIRST CREATED FROM A MOTHER'S EGG AND FATHER'S **SPERM** COMBINING.

FACT FLASH_ Not every cell contains DNA. Red blood cells and hair cells don't have a nucleus, so they don't carry DNA.

GENES

DNA spirals are long, but they are divided up into short sections called genes. Genes are like the pages in the DNA book. Each one has a different piece of information for the body about how it should work and grow. The gene section we are currently visiting determines the eye color of the body we are exploring.

DNA is made up of four types of chemicals, called adenine, thymine, cytosine, and guanine. They form pairs inside the DNA to make the steps on its spiral ladder shape. Adenine and thymine always pair together, and cytosine and guanine always match up. But it is the way they are ordered within each gene that codes the information.

THERE ARE AROUND 30,000 GENES IN EACH HUMAN CELL. EACH GENE SENDS INSTRUCTIONS TO THE CELL TO MAKE SPECIFIC PROTEINS. THESE PROTEINS PERFORM DIFFERENT TASKS, SUCH AS FIGHTING OFF INFECTIONS, DIGESTING FOOD, OR CARRYING NUTRIENTS AROUND THE BODY.

GENE MAP

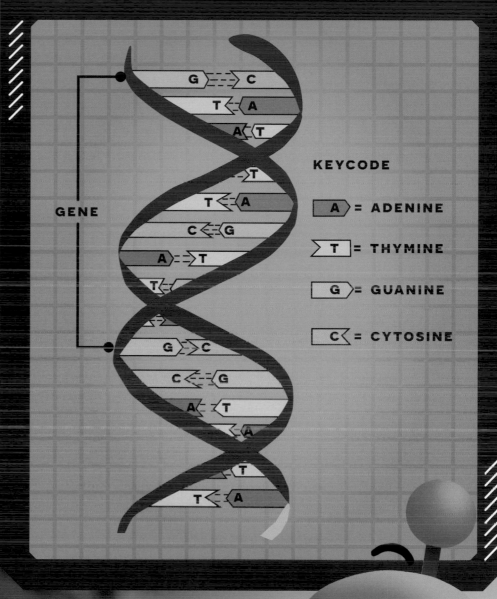

GENE

KEYCODE

A >	= ADENINE
> T	= THYMINE
G >	= GUANINE
C <	= CYTOSINE

Hallux is standing on a section of DNA containing the gene for eye color. The body we're exploring received a brown-eye gene from the mother's chromosome and a blue-eye gene from the father's chromosome. But brown-eye genes are dominant over blue-eye genes, so brown eyes are the resulting color for this body.

IT TAKES TWO

It's now time to look at two of the most specialized cells in the body – the ones that can create an entirely new human being! To study these cells, we have traveled to the uterus of the body – which means this body must be female (in case you've been wondering throughout the entire tour).

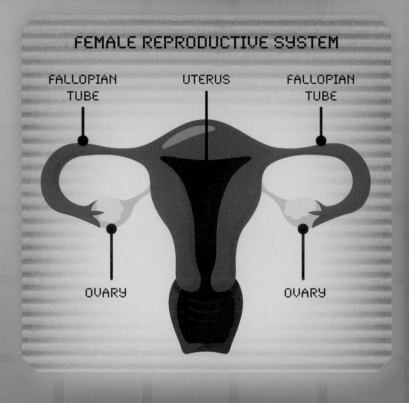

FEMALE REPRODUCTIVE SYSTEM

FALLOPIAN TUBE   UTERUS   FALLOPIAN TUBE

OVARY   OVARY

People who are born female have a uterus. It's a hollow, muscular organ located next to the bladder. Either side of the uterus are the ovaries, where tiny egg cells are made. When a female body reaches **puberty** (the transition from childhood to adulthood), an egg cell with 23 chromosomes is released from one of the ovaries every month.

The release of an egg from the ovary is called ovulation. Once the egg leaves the ovary, it travels down a narrow passage called the fallopian tube and enters the uterus. If the egg doesn't meet any sperm cells in the fallopian tube within 24 hours of its release, it dies and is removed from the body during the process of **menstruation**, about 14 days later.

BUT IF A SPERM CELL, ALSO WITH 23 CHROMOSOMES, MEETS THE EGG IN THE FALLOPIAN TUBE, THEN SOMETHING MAGICAL HAPPENS. THE TWO FUSE TOGETHER IN A PROCESS CALLED FERTILIZATION AND THE NEWLY FORMED CELL, WITH 46 CHROMOSOMES, DIVIDES INTO TWO. IT KEEPS DIVIDING, CREATING A CLUSTER OF CELLS, UNTIL IT ENTERS THE UTERUS AND IMPLANTS IN THE LINING. THIS IS THE BEGINNING OF A BRAND NEW HUMAN THAT WILL EVENTUALLY HAVE TRILLIONS OF CELLS!

FERTILIZATION

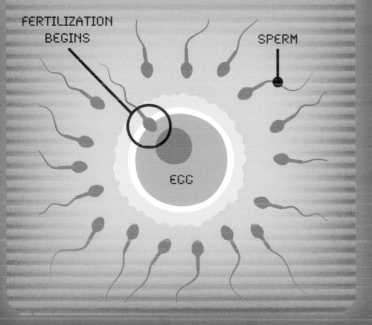

FERTILIZATION BEGINS

SPERM

EGG

A FERTILIZED EGG'S JOURNEY

FERTILIZED EGG TRAVELS ALONG THE FALLOPIAN TUBE

FERTILIZED EGG

OVARY

EGG IMPLANTS IN LINING OF UTERUS

Sperm cells are made within a male body's testicles, and they are shaped for swimming! All the genetic information is stored in the tip, while the tail helps move it up toward the ovaries, ready to meet the egg.

GESTATION

While we're here in the uterus, we're going to learn about **gestation**—this is what happens as a brand new human develops inside their mother before they're ready to be born. After a sperm fertilizes an egg, the cells divide, implant themselves in the uterus wall, and all the genes in the DNA in the chromosomes instruct the new body how to grow!

IN THE FIRST EIGHT WEEKS, THE DEVELOPING BABY IS CALLED AN EMBRYO, BUT AFTER THAT IT'S CALLED A FETUS. THE FETUS GROWS FAST, BUT IT TAKES NINE MONTHS BEFORE IT'S READY TO SURVIVE ON ITS OWN. UNTIL THEN, ALL ITS NEEDS AND NUTRITION ARE PROVIDED BY ITS MOTHER. THIS PERIOD OF TIME FOR THE MOTHER IS CALLED PREGNANCY.

PREGNANCY

PREGNANCY LASTS FOR ABOUT 280 DAYS, OR 40 WEEKS. IT'S DIVIDED INTO THREE PERIODS, CALLED TRIMESTERS.

FIRST TRIMESTER
WEEKS 1–12

SECOND TRIMESTER
WEEKS 13–28

UMBILICAL
CORD

FETUS

CERVIX   PLACENTA

FACT FLASH_ During the first trimester, the uterus is about the size of an orange, but by the third trimester it expands to the size of a watermelon.

A mother's body grows a whole new organ during pregnancy—the placenta. This special organ links the mother's bloodstream to that of the fetus via an umbilical cord. This means everything the fetus needs can be passed to it via the blood. It acts as the fetus's "lungs," supplying oxygen and removing carbon dioxide. It also removes waste, creates hormones, and helps to control and build the immune system.

**THIRD TRIMESTER
WEEKS 29–40**

After 40 weeks, the fetus is ready to be born, as there's no space left for it to grow inside! The uterus is a muscle, so it contracts to help push the fetus down, and the cervix at the entrance of the uterus widens just enough to allow the head to fit through it. When the fetus reaches the outside world, it can now be called a baby and it takes its first breath!

GOODBYE, BODY

Well, that's it! We've reached the end of the tour. We've seen many sights and created lots of memories, and hopefully you feel like you know a little more about yourself after this journey too! While we are leaving (for a well-earned rest), the body will continue working—every second of every minute of every day... for the rest of its life!

FACT FLASH_ The longest the human body has ever survived for is 122 years. A French lady called Jeanne Calment lived from 1875 to 1997.

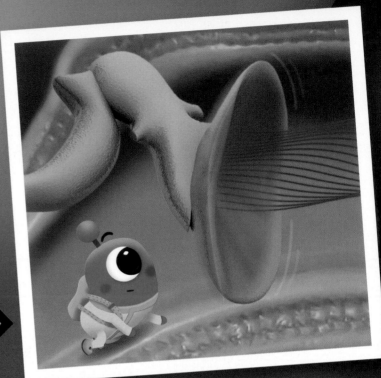

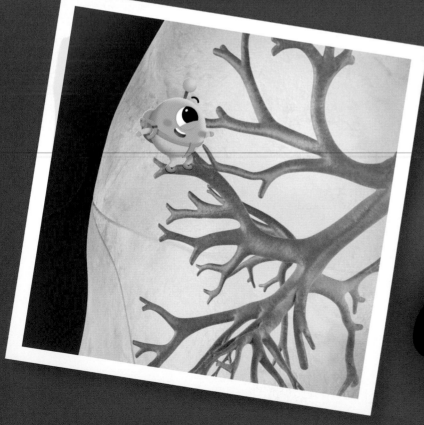

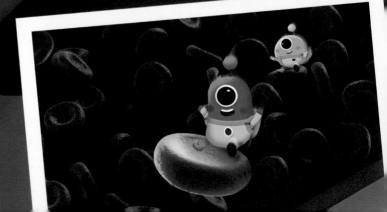

My favorite part of the tour was when we visited the ear—the hairs that pick up sound vibrations, the tiny bones that knock together, the sticky earwax, the buzz of the nerve cells. It was like being at a loud party!

I really enjoyed exploring the lungs. The branch-like bronchi and bronchiole airways made me feel like I was in a tranquil forest!

I'VE GOT A COUPLE OF FUN FACTS FOR YOU BEFORE WE WAVE GOODBYE... THE NAME DEWLAP COMES FROM THE FOLD OF LOOSE SKIN HANGING FROM THE NECK. AND HALLUX IS THE SCIENTIFIC NAME FOR THE BIG TOE!

Acid A substance that can sometimes be strong enough to dissolve other substances, such as the acid in the stomach that breaks down food.

Allergy An immune system reaction to a harmless substance such as food, plants, or dust.

Antibody A protein made by the immune system that can recognize and help destroy germs.

Antigen A molecule that the human body recognizes as foreign.

Artery A blood vessel that carries blood from the heart around the body.

Body system A collection of organs that work together to perform a specific role in the body, like digestion or circulation.

Bone The hard tissue that forms the body's skeleton.

Capillary The smallest type of blood vessel, which connects arteries to veins.

Carbon dioxide A waste gas produced by the body, made up of carbon and oxygen.

Cartilage Tough, flexible tissue found in the body, especially where bones meet.

Cell A tiny building block that makes up living things.

Chromosome A structure that carries information about the body, found in most cells. Chromosomes contain DNA.

Communication The act of giving or receiving information.

DNA Stands for deoxyribonucleic acid. A long molecule found in chromosomes, DNA is made up of a chain of chemicals that contain the code for information about the body. Sections of DNA are called genes.

Enzyme A chemical that can build up or break down molecules and speed up chemical reactions.

Gene The section of DNA that carries the code for specific traits, like hair and eye color.

Gestation The period of time when a baby develops inside their mother.

Gland A group of cells that produce and release into the body a substance with a particular job to do.

Glucose The main type of sugar found in the body, which is used as a source of energy for cells.

Hormone A chemical, made by the body, that helps control body processes, such as growth.

Infection An illness caused by germs entering and multiplying inside the body.

Joint A place in the body where bones meet.

Ligament A strong band of tissue that holds bones together at a joint.

Lymph A clear fluid that flows around the body through vessels before being returned to the bloodstream.

Medicine A substance taken into the body to help treat illness, injury, or pain.

Membrane A thin, soft, flexible layer that surrounds cells and tissues.

Menstruation The process of blood and tissue being expelled from a female's body once a month when the uterus sheds its lining.

Microorganisms Simple living things that are too small to be seen with the eye, such as bacteria and viruses.

Mind The part of the brain that thinks, feels, understands, and remembers.

Mineral A naturally occurring chemical that the body needs in tiny amounts to function, such as iron.

Molecule The smallest unit of a substance, made up of atoms joined by chemical bonds.

Mucus A thick, sticky substance that coats and moistens the lining of passages in the body, like the throat, lungs, and intestines.

Muscle A tissue in the body made of muscle fibers, which can contract to produce movement.

Muscle fiber A single muscle cell that can contract and relax.

Nerve A group of nerve cells in the nervous system that carry messages around the body.

Nucleus The control center of a cell. It contains chromosomes made up of DNA.

Nutrient A substance taken into the body as food that is needed for healthy growth, development, and energy.

Odor Molecules carried in the air that trigger the body's sense of smell in the nose.

Organ A group of tissues that work together to perform a specific function, like the heart.

Oxygen A gas found in air that the body needs to survive.

Puberty The period of time when the body begins to develop from a child into an adult, controlled by hormones.

Receptor A sensory cell that reacts to a stimulus such as light or heat and activates a nerve to send a message to the brain.

Reflex The involuntary (automatic) reaction of the body to something.

Reproduce The way living things produce offspring.

Saliva The liquid produced by glands in the mouth to help soften food. Saliva is made of water, chemicals, and enzymes.

Scar A mark left on the skin after a cut or wound has healed and new skin has formed.

Sense One of the ways the body experiences its surroundings in order to react to them. The five main senses are touch, smell, taste, sight, and hearing.

Sound When something vibrates and creates waves of energy in the air that the body can hear via the ears.

Sperm A cell made only in male bodies that can fertilize (join with) a female egg cell in order to create a baby.

Sweat A liquid made by glands in the skin when the body is hot and needs to cool itself down.

Tendon A strong, stretchy band of tissue that connects muscle to bone.

Tissue A group of the same cells that work together to do a specific job.

Toxin A poison produced by a living thing that causes harm.

Vaccination A substance put into the body to teach the immune system how to respond to and fight off a particular infection in the future.

Vein A blood vessel that carries blood back from the body to the heart.

Vitamin A chemical found in food that the body needs in order to function.

PICTURE CREDITS

The publisher would like to thank the following for their kind permission to reproduce their images:

Key: t=top, b=bottom, c=center, r=right, l=left, bg=background

123RF
7activestudio: 94 c, 102–103 main image / crystallight: 116–117 main image / Eraxion: 112–113 main image / exploderasi: 42–43 main image

Alamy
MedicalRF.com: 38–39 main image / Science Photo Library: 40 c

Getty
spanteldotru: front cover main image

Shutterstock
32 pixels: 82–83 bg / Aldona Griskeviciene: 69 main image, 72 tr, 73 tl, t, cr, cl and c / Alila Medical Media: 123 t / Anatomy Image: 74–75 main image / Andrea Danti: 114c, 115 bl and c / Axel_Kock: 88 t and b, 89 t / Chawalit Banpot: 28 t, 29 t and c / Choksawatdikorn: 76 t / CLIPAREA: 21 t / Crevis: 31 cr, 41 tl / crystal light: 106–107 main image / daily_creativity: 6–7 main image, 110–111 main image / Design_Cells: 26–27 main image / eranicle: 11 tr / EreborMountain: 36 b / Explode: 18–19 main image, 67 br, 70–71 main image / Foxstudio: 83 b / fusebulb: 54 t and c, 55 t, 60 t / GS1981: 24 bl / Gunita Reine: 16–17 main image, 20 b, 70–71 bg, 71 c / HorenkO: 10–11 bg, 14–15 bg, 38–39 bg, 42–43 bg, 50–51 bg, 52–53 bg, 56–57 bg, 106–107 bg, 126–127 bg / Ihor: 80–81 bg, 122–123 bg / jessicahyde: 40–41 bg / Kateryna Kon: 10 b, 31 tr, 48 bl, 98 cr, 99 tr, 114 t, c and b, 115 t and b, back cover / KateStudio: 12 bl / Kurteev Gennadii: 129 t / Madrock24: 56 c, 87 tl, back cover / Magic mine: 44–45 main image, 72–73 main image / MattLphotography: 8 l, 12 c, 13 t and b, 28 b, 128 t and c / Maxx-Studio: 32–33 main image, 139 br / MDGRPHCS: 84–85 main image, 92–93 main image / Mesa Studios: 60 b, 79 c, 85 tr / mybox: 68 main image / Nathapol Kongseang: 120–121 main image / nobeastsofierce: 54 t, c and b, 55 t, 99 tl, 132–133 main image / Pepe Gallardo: 40 t, 41 tr and b / peterschreiber.media: 61 c and b, 128 b, 138 br / Phonlamai Photo: 98 cl / PixieMe: 108–109 main image / Roman3dArt: 30–31 main image / Rost9: 20–21 bg / S K Chavan: 86 main image / sciencepics: 64–65 main image, 86 t and c / SciePro: 8–9 main image and l, 10–11 main image, 12 t, 14–15 main image, 34–35 main image, 36–37 main image, 46–47 main image, 48–49 main image, 50–51 main image, 56–57 main image, 58–59 main image, 60 b, 61 t and b, 62–63 main image, 66–67 main image, 74 l, 77 t, 78–79 main image, 80–81 main image, 82–83 main image, 86 b, 87 bl, 90–91 main image, 91 tr, 93 c, 94–95 bg, 96–97 main image, 98–99 bg, 100–101 bg, 104–105 main image, 118 tr, 118–119 main image, 122–123 main image, 124 t, 124–125 main image, 126–127 main image, 130–131 main image, 131 c, 138 bl and br, back cover / Stock Image Vendor: 138 t / supergalactic: 62 c and b, 63 cr, 95 tr, back cover / Tanawat Thipmontha: 90–91 bg / Vendor: 22–23 main image, 24–25 main image / Volodymyr Horbovyy: 64–65 bg, 102–103 bg / xpixel: 33 c, 139 br / Yurchanka Siarhei: 124 c, 129 b / background elements by Qvils: 10, 13, 15, 16, 34–35, 37, 43, 44–45, 53, 65, 72–73, 75, 76–77, 78–79, 82–83, 86–87, 91, 92–93, 98–99, 103, 111, 113, 115, 116, 121, 126–127, 134–135, 137

All other images shutterstock.com